Harvard
Business
Review

ON

THE INNOVATIVE ENTERPRISE

THE HARVARD BUSINESS REVIEW PAPERBACK SERIES

The series is designed to bring today's managers and professionals the fundamental information they need to stay competitive in a fast-moving world. From the preeminent thinkers whose work has defined an entire field to the rising stars who will redefine the way we think about business, here are the leading minds and landmark ideas that have established the *Harvard Business Review* as required reading for ambitious businesspeople in organizations around the globe.

Other books in the series:

Harvard Business Review Interviews with CEOs

Harvard Business Review on Advances in Strategy

Harvard Business Review on Becoming a High Performance Manager

Harvard Business Review on Brand Management

Harvard Business Review on Breakthrough Leadership

Harvard Business Review on Breakthrough Thinking

Harvard Business Review on Business and the Environment

Harvard Business Review on the Business Value of IT

Harvard Business Review on Change

Harvard Business Review on Compensation

Harvard Business Review on Corporate Governance

Harvard Business Review on Corporate Strategy

Harvard Business Review on Crisis Management

Harvard Business Review on Culture and Change

Harvard Business Review on Customer Relationship Management

Harvard Business Review on Decision Making

Harvard Business Review on Effective Communication

Harvard Business Review on Entrepreneurship

Harvard Business Review on Finding and Keeping the Best People

Other books in the series (continued):

Harvard Business Review on Innovation

Harvard Business Review on Knowledge Management

Harvard Business Review on Leadership

Harvard Business Review on Leading in Turbulent Times

Harvard Business Review on Managing Diversity

Harvard Business Review on Managing High Tech Industries

Harvard Business Review on Managing People

Harvard Business Review on Managing Uncertainty

Harvard Business Review on Managing the Value Chain

Harvard Business Review on Managing Your Career

Harvard Business Review on Marketing

Harvard Business Review on Measuring Corporate Performance

Harvard Business Review on Mergers and Acquisitions

Harvard Business Review on Negotiation and Conflict Resolution

Harvard Business Review on Nonprofits

Harvard Business Review on Organizational Learning

Harvard Business Review on Strategic Alliances

Harvard Business Review on Strategies for Growth

Harvard Business Review on Turnarounds

Harvard Business Review on Work and Life Balance

Harvard Business Review

ON

THE INNOVATIVE

ENTERPRISE

A HARVARD BUSINESS REVIEW PAPERBACK

The *Harvard Business Review* articles in this collection are available as individual reprints. Discounts apply to quantity purchases. For information and ordering, please contact Customer Service, Harvard Business School Publishing, Boston, MA 02163. Telephone: (617) 783-7500 or (800) 988-0886, 8 A.M. to 6 P.M. Eastern Time, Monday through Friday. Fax: (617) 783-7555, 24 hours a day. E-mail: custserv@hbsp.harvard.edu

Library of Congress Cataloging-in-Publication Data
Harvard business review on the innovative enterprise.
     p. cm. — (The Harvard business review paperback series)
     Includes index.
     ISBN 1-59139-130-X (alk. paper)
     1. Technological innovations. 2. Creative ability in business. 3. Research, Inudstrial. I. Harvard business review. II. Series.
     HD45 .H343 2003
     658.4´063—dc21
                                         2002152617
                                            CIP

The paper used in this publication meets the requirements of the American National Standard for Permanence of Paper for Publications and Documents in Libraries and Archives Z39.48-1992.

Contents

Harvard
Business
Review

ON

THE INNOVATIVE ENTERPRISE

Creativity Under the Gun

TERESA M. AMABILE, CONSTANCE N. HADLEY, AND STEVEN J. KRAMER

Executive Summary

IF YOU'RE LIKE MOST MANAGERS, you've worked with people who swear they do their most creative work under tight deadlines. You may use pressure as a management technique, believing it will spur people on to great leaps of insight. You may even manage yourself this way. If so, are you right?

Not necessarily, these researchers say. There are instances where ingenuity flourishes under extreme time pressure—for instance, a NASA team within hours comes up with a primitive but effective fix for the failing air filtration system aboard Apollo 13. But when creativity is under the gun, it usually ends up getting killed, the authors say. They recently took a close look at how people experience time pressure, collecting and analyzing more than 9,000 daily diary entries from individuals who were working on projects that required high

1

levels of creativity and measuring their ability to innovate under varying levels of time pressure.

The authors describe common characteristics of time
pressure and outline four working environments under
which creativity may or may not flourish. High-pressure
days that still yield creativity are full of focus and meaningful urgency—people feel like they are *on a mission*.
High-pressure days that yield no creativity lack such
focus—people feel like they are *on a treadmill*, forced to
switch gears often. On low-pressure days that yield creativity, people feel like they are *on an expedition*—exploring ideas rather than just identifying problems. And on
low-pressure days that yield no creative thinking, people
work *on autopilot*—doing their jobs without engaging too
deeply.

Managers should avoid extreme time pressure when
possible; after all, complex cognitive processing takes
time. For when they can't, the authors suggest ways to
mollify its effects.

T RULY BREAKTHROUGH IDEAS rarely hatch overnight. Consider, for example, Charles Darwin's theory of
evolution, which had a protracted evolution of its own.
Darwin spent decades reading scientific literature, making voyages on the HMS *Beagle* to the Galápagos and
other exotic destinations, carrying out painstakingly
detailed observations, and producing thousands of pages
of notes on those observations and his ideas for explain-
ing them. It's inconceivable that his breakthrough would
have occurred if he'd tried to rush it. In business, too,
there are striking examples of the value of having relatively unstructured, unpressured time to create and

develop new ideas. Scientists working at AT&T's legendary Bell Labs, operating under its corporate philosophy that big ideas take time, produced world-changing innovations including the transistor and the laser beam. Their ingenuity earned the researchers several Nobel prizes. They, like Darwin, had the time to think creatively.

But we can all point to examples where creativity seemed to be sparked by extreme time pressure. In 1970, during Apollo 13's flight to the moon, a crippling explosion occurred on board, damaging the air filtration system and leading to a dangerous buildup of carbon dioxide in the cabin. If the system could not be fixed or replaced, the astronauts would be dead within a few hours. Back at NASA mission control in Houston, virtually all engineers, scientists, and technicians immediately focused their attention on the problem. Working with a set of materials identical to those on board the spacecraft, they desperately tried to build a filtration system that the astronauts might be able to replicate. Every conceivable material was considered, including the cover of a flight procedure manual. With little time to spare, they came up with something that was ugly, inelegant, and far from perfect but that seemed like it just might do the job. The engineers quickly conveyed the design with enough clarity that the cognitively impaired astronauts were, almost unbelievably, able to build the filter. It worked, and three lives were saved.

The business examples of creativity under pressure are decidedly less dramatic than that, but they abound as well. The lauded design firm Ideo has put its innovative spin on personal computers, medical equipment, automotive electronics, toys, and even animatronic movie robots—and many of the new designs for those products were drawn up in three months or less. If you're like most managers, you have almost certainly worked with people who swear that they do their most creative work under tight deadlines. You may use pressure as a management technique, believing that it will spur people on to great leaps of insight. You may even manage yourself this way. If so, are you right?

Based on our research, the short answer is "no." When creativity is under the gun, it usually ends up getting killed. Although time pressure may drive people to work more and get more done, and may even make them *feel* more creative, it actually causes them, in general, to think less creatively. Of course, the short answer is not the whole story. Let's take a look at what time pressure is, how it feels when people experience it at work, and the different ways it can be managed to enhance creativity.

Fighting the Clock

Maria was a software developer on a team charged with creating an on-line system through which health care providers could access vital information about certain high-risk patients. It was critical that the new system be error-proof because the targeted patients were elderly or severely disabled individuals; in life-threatening situations, accurate information about them had to be communicated instantly. Unfortunately, the original contract for the project had vastly underestimated the time required to develop it. As a result, Maria and her team found themselves under extreme time pressure as the deadline approached. (Maria's identity, like all individual, project, and corporate identities in this article, has been disguised.)

The team was working almost around the clock, even though it was becoming clearer with each passing day that the complex technical problems it encountered simply could not be solved adequately within the original time frame. Yet senior management, as well as the project leader, pressed the team to meet the deadline, no matter what. Maria recorded her experiences during this time in a daily diary:

"At 7:30 this morning, my team leader asked me what my game plan was for the day and if I could be available for a rollout meeting. I wrote out on a flip chart what I thought needed to be done today, looked at the list, and told him it was two or three days of work. Now, as I am burned out and preparing to leave for the day, I look at the flip chart and realize that, at best, 20% of the work has been accomplished. This one-day list is really a four- or five-day list. The thing that most sticks in my mind from the entire day is that blasted flip chart with so little crossed off."

A few days later, Maria seemed even closer to the end of her rope:

"I told my supervisor that the hours I am working are completely unacceptable and that I planned to leave the company if this continued to be the norm on projects here. The look on his face was a bit aghast. Was he really shocked? Could this possibly be a surprise? All afternoon I felt physically drained, as if I were running on low blood sugar. I slept very poorly last night, several hours awake in the middle of the night. I feel physically exhausted again right now—lack of mental clarity, lack of motivation about the project."

Maria wasn't alone in her sense of the extreme time pressure the group was working under. Richard, another member of the team, kept his own diary during this period and had this to say:

"The team leader announced that the project's core hours—when everyone is expected to be in the office and working—have been extended: 'They are now 8 AM to 7 PM, and don't make social plans for the next three weekends, as we will likely be working.' This project is now officially a death march in my mind. I can't fathom how much work we have left, how severely we underestimated this project, and how complex this dog has become. At every turn, we uncover more things that are unsettled, incomplete, or way more complex than we ever thought."

We collected more than 9,000 such diary entries in a recent study of 177 employees in seven U.S. companies. Our objective was to look deeply at how people experienced time pressure day to day as they worked on projects that required high levels of inventiveness, while also measuring their ability to think creatively under such pressure. Specifically, we asked each of the participants— most of whom were highly educated knowledge workers—to complete a diary form on-line in which they rated several aspects of their work and their work environment that day, including how much time pressure they felt. In a separate section of the form, we also asked them to describe something that stood out in their minds about that day, and we carefully analyzed those short entries for evidence of creative thinking. (See "Trapping Creativity in the Wild" at the end of this article for a detailed description of our research method, including our study's specific definition of "creative thinking.")

What we saw in those diary entries was both fascinating and sobering. Many of the people in our study reported experiences similar to Maria's: They often felt overworked, fragmented, and burned out. At the most basic level, then, we found support for recent observations in the popular press that Americans are feeling a time crunch at work, creating what one *Newsweek* reporter called a nation of "the quick, or the dead-tired." The problem has been with us for some time. As early as 1995, *U.S. News & World Report* described a nationwide poll showing that more than half of Americans wanted more free time, even if it meant earning less money. And In 1996, according to a *Wall Street Journal–NBC News* survey, 75% of those people earning more than $100,000 a year cited managing their time as a bigger problem than managing their money.

Time pressure has become a fact of life for the American worker. On the average day, our study participants reported feeling "moderate" time pressure—and that was the average. A great many of the participants' workdays were characterized by "extremely" high levels of time pressure. "Today I realized that our time to get ready for the upcoming presentations was almost nonexistent," wrote one participant in a fairly typical entry. Another, in a different company, lamented that, "Overnight, I had to come up with a fully detailed plan for the remainder of the development phase, to let us know how far behind we were."

Perhaps not surprisingly, although our participants said time pressure was rather high most of the time, we noticed a trend whereby time pressure seemed to build as work projects went from early to later stages; as with Maria's project, people felt more and more pressed for time as deadlines approached. Interestingly, we also observed a slight trend in time-pressure changes during the week: The time pressure started out relatively low on Mondays, increased through the week to a peak on

Thursdays, and decreased on Fridays. This may be because managers' expectations for productivity are somewhat lower on Mondays and Fridays. Or perhaps it's simply that, on the days bracketing the weekend, people are already (or still) in a weekend mind-set and less subject to feeling the time pressure that exists. We also found that people were more likely to report high levels of time pressure on days when they were traveling for work or working off-site. It's possible that people try to pack more work into such days to minimize the total time spent away from the office. And, of course, the many hassles of travel itself undoubtedly contribute to feelings of being pressed.

Energy and Frustration

As described in the diaries, the days when our study participants felt extreme time pressure were noticeably different from the days when they felt less time pressure. People tended to work more hours and were involved in a greater number of activities, having to switch gears more often, on time-pressured days. That provides us with our first clue about how time pressure might affect creativity—a clue to which we will return later.

People experienced different feelings as time pressure increased, but we can't simply say that they felt better or worse. It was a mixed bag. At first, people felt more involved in and challenged by their work: "I am under a lot of pressure to start up the manufacturing machine for our new product this week. . . . I was actually happy to run to the hardware stores for hose fittings and bolts. For the first time, I feel like we are truly making real progress." And, in surprising contrast to Maria's reaction of feeling drained, people generally felt more energized under high pressure. As one diarist reported, "We are

three-quarters of the way there! I really enjoy seeing the
team pull together."

But some people also experienced deep frustration as
time pressure increased: "I frequently feel I am swimming
upstream on this project and always buried with work." In
particular, they seemed frustrated by constant distractions from other team members on time-pressured days.
One of our study participants told a particularly vivid
story about his frustration with a colleague:

"We had a meeting about what is going wrong with
the filtration program and how to come to an acceptable
level of understanding and information gathering. As
usual, Paul, Emilio, Sarah, and I were going at breakneck
speed trying to make sure we're all pulling together. But
Raj could only repeatedly say, 'But what part of my job
don't you want me to do, if you expect me to do that?' He
was argumentative and negative, and all I could think
was, 'Stop it!' I was able to control myself and didn't
scream at him, but I was close."

When we look at the whole picture of how people
were experiencing time pressure, it seems they were
working hard, spending long hours on the job, and sometimes feeling jazzed about what they were doing. But at
the same time, there was a lot of frustration—another
clue that will help us understand time pressure's effects
on creativity.

The Pressure Trap

Our study indicates that the more time pressure people
feel on a given day, the less likely they will be to think
creatively. Surprisingly, though, people seem to be largely
unaware of this phenomenon. In their assessments of
their own creativity each day, the participants in our
study generally perceived themselves as having been

more creative when time pressure was high. Sadly, their diaries gave the lie to those self-assessments. There was clearly less and less creative thinking in evidence as time pressure increased.

Moreover, the drop in creative thinking was most apparent when time pressure was at its worst. In the daily diary form, participants were asked to rate the time pressure they felt on a scale of one to seven, with seven being the highest level of pressure. On the days rated a seven, people were 45% less likely to think creatively than they were on any of the lower-pressure days.

Managers might think that the occasional uncreative day is simply the price paid for keeping work on a highly productive schedule. If your creative juices freeze up on a particularly busy Thursday, they might argue, you'll be able to get back to creativity on Friday when the demands have died down a bit. But maybe not. To our surprise, more time pressure on a certain day meant less creative thinking that day, the next day, *and* the day after that. In other words, whether because of exhaustion or enduring postpressure cognitive paralysis, our study participants seemed to experience a "pressure hangover" that lasted a couple of days at least.

That lingering time-pressure effect showed up whether we examined time pressure day to day or over longer periods. The higher the overall sense of time pressure that participants felt during the first week of their projects, the lower the level of creative thinking we saw from them during the first half of their projects (a period that varied from three weeks to four months). And the higher the overall sense of time pressure at the midpoint, the lower the level of creative thinking in the second half.

Why does time pressure have this dampening effect on creativity? Psychological research over the past 30 years, along with theories about how creativity happens, can help to explain. Psychologists have long believed that creativity results from the formation of a large number of associations in the mind, followed by the selection of associations that may be particularly interesting and useful. In a sense, it's as if the mind is throwing a bunch of balls into the cognitive space, juggling them around until they collide in interesting ways. The process has a certain playful quality to it; in fact, Einstein once referred to creativity as "combinatorial play." If associations are made between concepts that are rarely combined—that is, if balls that don't normally come near one another collide—the ultimate novelty of the solution will be greater.

Considerable research, drawn from experiments and from observations of creative activities, supports this view of the creative process. And some recent research suggests that the success of the combinatorial process depends both on having sufficient time to create the balls to juggle—exploring concepts and learning things that might somehow be useful—and having sufficient time to devote to the actual juggling. For example, one study we and our colleagues conducted found that people who allocate more time to exploratory behaviors while doing a task produce work that is rated by experts as more creative. Another study found that simply having a few minutes to think through a task—studying the materials, playing around with them—can lead to more creativity than having to dive into the task cold. So we have still more clues about how being under the gun might affect the creative process.

Protecting Creativity

Even though time pressure seems to undermine creative thinking in general, there are striking exceptions. We know, from our own study and from anecdotal evidence, that people can and do come up with ingenious solutions under desperately short time frames. What makes the difference? It's time to put the clues together.

When we compared the diary entries from the time-pressured days when creative thinking happened to the entries from the time-pressured days when no creative thinking happened, we found that the creative days featured a particular—and rather rare—set of working conditions. Above all else, these days were marked by a sense of focus. People were able to concentrate on a single work activity for a significant portion of the day. As one diarist jubilantly declared: "The event of the day was that I had no standout events. I was able to concentrate on the project at hand without interruptions." This focus was often hard-won, as the individuals or their managers went to great lengths to protect their work from interruptions and other disturbances: "There were so many interruptions for chitchat that I couldn't get any decent work accomplished. I eventually had to go work very quietly in another room to get some of it done."

Indeed, this sense of focus implies some degree of isolation. On the time-pressured days that still yielded creative thinking, we noted that collaboration was limited. When it happened, it was somewhat more likely to be done in a concentrated way—for instance, working with another individual rather than in a group: "I had a chance to talk at the end of the day with Susan. She helped confirm that the path I was taking was right and helped me figure out some of the differences in the codes. Her help will keep me going."

Another key condition for achieving creativity on the high-pressure days was interpreting the time pressure as meaningful urgency. People understood why solving a problem or completing a job was crucial, and they bought into that urgency, feeling as though they were *on a mission*. (See the exhibit "The Time-Pressure/Creativity Matrix" for a summary of the work conditions our study participants experienced.) They were involved in their work and felt positively challenged by it. The sense of urgency and the ability to focus are probably related, for two reasons. If people believe that their work is vitally important, they may be more willing and able to ignore a variety of distractions in their workdays. Meanwhile, managers who share this sense of urgency may free people from less-essential tasks. This was clearly the case in the Apollo 13 mission: All nonessential work was abandoned until the air filtration problem was solved and the astronauts were returned home safely.

But when this protected focus was missing on time-pressured days—and it very often was—people felt more like they were *on a treadmill*. On these days, our diarists reported a more extreme level of time pressure even though they were not working more hours, and they felt much more distracted. When recording the number of different activities they performed, they were likely to use words like "several," "many," and "too numerous to count." They were pulled in too many directions, unable to focus on a single activity for any significant period of time. One diarist, paraphrasing the oft-repeated lament, said: "The faster I run, the behinder I get."

Our first clue, that people might have to switch gears more often under time pressure, underlies this treadmill condition; many things are clamoring for people's attention simultaneously. Remember, too, our clue that feelings of time pressure are associated with frustration, especially frustration with other members of a team. We suspect that interruptions contribute to that frustration.

The Time-Pressure/Creativity Matrix

Our study suggests that time pressure affects creativity in different ways depending on whether the environment allows people to focus on their work, conveys a sense of meaningful urgency about the tasks at hand, or stimulates or undermines creative thinking in other ways.

		Time Pressure	
		low	**high**
Likelihood of Creative Thinking	**high**	Creative thinking under low time pressure is more likely when people feel as if they are **on an expedition**. They: • show creative thinking that is more oriented toward generating or exploring ideas than identifying problems. • tend to collaborate with one person rather than with a group.	Creative thinking under extreme time pressure is more likely when people feel as if they are **on a mission**. They: • can focus on one activity for a significant part of the day because they are undisturbed or protected. • believe that they are doing important work and report feeling positively challenged by and involved in the work. • show creative thinking that is equally oriented toward identifying problems and generating or exploring ideas.
	low	Creative thinking under low time pressure is unlikely when people feel as if they are **on autopilot**. They: • receive little encouragement from senior management to be creative. • tend to have more meetings and discussions with groups rather than with individuals. • engage in less collaborative work overall.	Creative thinking under extreme time pressure is unlikely when people feel as if they are **on a treadmill**. They: • feel distracted. • experience a highly fragmented workday, with many different activities. • don't get the sense that the work they are doing is important. • feel more pressed for time than when they are "on a mission" even though they work the same number of hours. • tend to have more meetings and discussions with groups rather than with individuals. • experience lots of last-minute changes in their plans and schedules.

Other evidence adds to the picture of a distracted, disturbed, confusing environment on treadmill days. People had many more meetings and discussions with groups rather than with individuals. Moreover, they often had to cope with last-minute changes to schedules and plans. In many ways, they seemed to be operating under greater uncertainty: "At the meeting, we discovered that the work we have done to date may have to be completely redone because of a decision made by upper management to change the way the new system will process customer orders." On these low-focus, time-pressured days, people weren't very likely to see what they were doing as important or to feel a meaningful sense of urgency to complete a project or task.

Did an absence of time pressure guarantee that people would be more creative? Certainly not. Under any level of time pressure, low or high, reports of creative thinking were relatively rare; they showed up in only about 5% of the 9,000-plus daily diary reports. Under low time pressure, the differences in whether creativity happened or not seem to lie in the way people were spending their days. Most noticeably, when people exhibited creativity in the absence of time pressure, they were more oriented toward exploring and generating new ideas than identifying problems to be solved. (Remember our clue from the psychological literature on combinatorial play.) People behaved as if they were *on an expedition.* In addition, if people in this condition worked with someone else, they tended to spend the day (or part of it) collaborating with only one other person; collaboration with many people was rare. Having a single focal point to bounce new ideas off of might help people stay oriented toward the work on these more relaxed days, in contrast to having many "playmates" at once.

Finally, of course, there were days when people didn't feel under much time pressure and didn't show any evidence of creative thinking. They seemed to be doing their jobs, putting one foot in front of the other, without engaging too deeply in what was happening. They behaved as though they were *on autopilot*. On these days, there was a generally low level of collaborative work, although there were more meetings and discussions that involved groups rather than individuals. And people felt the least encouragement from high-level management to do creative work. Perhaps if creativity had been encouraged more, these individuals would have made better use of their relatively low-pressure days.

Lessons for Management—and Self-Management

Our research focused on knowledge workers—people who, according to researcher Leslie Perlow, are most likely to suffer from a "time famine" in contemporary American organizations. These are the people from whom we need and expect the highest levels of creativity; they are developing the products, services, and organizations of tomorrow. They are also the people who are most handicapped in their quest to be creative.

There's no doubt that creative thinking is possible under high—even extreme—time pressure. But this seems to be likely only in a situation that, research suggests, is not the norm in modern organizations: being able to become deeply immersed, and stay deeply immersed, in an important, urgent problem. Given the demands in most organizations for communication and

process checks, as well as the prevalence of highly inter-
dependent work roles, protected creativity time does not
occur naturally. What,
then, can managers do to
minimize the negative
effects of time pressure
and use it appropriately
in the service of creativity? What can each of us
do to maintain our own creativity in today's pressured
organizations?

Don't be fooled into thinking that time pressure will, in itself, spur creativity. That's a powerful illusion but an illusion nonetheless.

Our first suggestion is the obvious one: Avoid extreme
time pressure whenever possible, particularly if you are
looking for high levels of
learning, exploration, idea
generation, and experi-
mentation with new con-
cepts. Don't be fooled into
thinking that time pres-
sure will, in itself, spur creativity. That's a powerful
illusion but an illusion
nonetheless. Complex cognitive processing takes time,
and, without some reasonable time for that processing,
creativity is almost impossible.

Signing a contract that promises to deliver items to a client by a certain date, without careful scoping of what the project will likely involve, can lead to the treadmill mentality.

Of course, it would be foolish to think that the ideal
for creativity is a complete absence of time pressure on a
particular work project. Given the demands that modern
life puts on people, it's too likely that other things would
steal attention from the project—the urgent would drive
out the important—and nothing would be accomplished.
Moreover, it would be easy for people to slip into autopilot mode if there were no sense of urgency. Our research

suggests that low time pressure doesn't necessarily foster creative thinking—but that it can do so when people are encouraged to learn, to play with ideas, and to develop something truly new. Consider the creativity-shielding practices at 3M. For many years, that innovation power-house has had a tradition of protecting 15% of the work-week for creative endeavors. All its R&D scientists devote that time to exploring whatever new ideas or pet projects most intrigue them personally, even if those ideas and projects are far afield from their assigned work.

For most companies, the best way to avoid undue time pressure is to articulate goals at all levels of the organization that are realistic and carefully planned, avoiding the optimism bias that plagues a lot of corporate planning. Announcing that a certain number of new products will be developed in the coming year, without a sense of the feasibility of that goal, will probably cause extreme time pressure to ripple through the organization—right down to the people who are actually supposed to be coming up with the ideas for those products. Signing a contract that promises to deliver items to a client by a certain date, without careful scoping of what the project will likely involve, can lead to the treadmill mentality that we saw on Maria's team. People may continue to advance the work, but they won't have the creative insights that will send the project leapfrogging ahead to truly exciting solutions.

In situations where time pressure can't be avoided, managers should focus on protecting time-pressured people who are supposed to be doing creative work from interruptions, distractions, and unrelated demands for a significant portion of each workweek. This concentration on "real work" can reduce the time fragmentation that we saw in so many of our participants' daily diaries.

Perlow's research in a high-tech firm, as reported in her book *Finding Time: How Corporations, Individuals, and Families Can Benefit from New Work Practices* (Cornell University Press, 1997), showed that engineers who agreed to give one another such uninterrupted quiet time during specified periods each day were able to get more done on their projects and felt better about their workdays. Her research also suggested, unfortunately, that it is difficult to sustain such a major change in workday norms without deep cultural change in the organization.

Creativity can also be supported under time-pressured conditions if managers can help people understand why tight time frames are necessary. It's much easier to feel that you are on a mission if you accept that there is an important, urgent need for the work you are doing, rather than feeling that an arbitrary deadline has been handed down simply to make you run ever faster on your treadmill. Our research suggests that managers should also encourage one-on-one collaborations and discussions, avoiding an excess of the obligatory group meetings that may contribute to feelings of fragmentation and wasted time. Finally, people may be better able to concentrate on their work if managers minimize abrupt changes in scheduled activities and plans.

In short, the key to protecting creative activity—including your own—is to offset the effects of extreme time pressure. The obvious way to do that is to reduce the time pressure. But in cases where it is unavoidable, its negative effects can be softened somewhat by getting your people and yourself in the mind-set of being on a mission—sharing a sense that the work is vital and the urgency legitimate. It also means ruthlessly guarding protected blocks of the workweek, shielding staff from the distractions and interruptions that are the normal condition of organizational life. The best situation for creativity is not to be under the gun. But if you can't manage that, at least learn to dodge the bullets.

Trapping Creativity in the Wild

MANY OF THE FINDINGS WE REPORT in this article are drawn from a study of time pressure and creativity that we recently conducted with Jennifer Mueller of Yale School of Management and William Simpson and Lee Fleming, both of Harvard Business School. That study included data from 177 employees who were members of 22 project teams from seven U.S. companies within three industries (chemical, high tech, and consumer products). More than 85% of the participants had college degrees, and many had graduate education. In order to be included in the study, a team had to be identified by senior management as working on a project where creativity was both possible and desirable. In other words, these projects, and our participants, were considered the "creative lifeblood" of their organizations. We believed that we could better understand what these people were experiencing each day, and what was really influencing their creativity, if we tracked what was happening in real time.

To accomplish this, we e-mailed each member of each team a brief daily questionnaire throughout the entire course of their projects. We asked them to fill it out and return it to us at the end of each workday. Somewhat amazingly, 75% of the questionnaires that we sent out were returned completed even though some of the projects we followed lasted more than six months. This yielded the very high number of returns (9,134) that we analyzed in this study. The questionnaires contained several numerical-scale items about the work and the work environment, including one that asked participants to rate the day's time pressure on a seven-point scale. A similar item asked them to rate the creativity of their work that day.

The most interesting part of the questionnaire was the narrative diary entry, in which we asked participants to briefly describe one event that stood out in their minds from the day—anything at all that related to the project, the team, or their work. (We did not ask them to focus on creativity.) Because we asked for just one standout event each day, the diaries do not present a comprehensive account of everything that happened that day. We assume, though, that they are a representative sample of the important things that were happening. And although we saw some clear patterns in the results, further research will be necessary to determine definitively what is causing what.

The diary entries provided rich information about what people were doing and experiencing each day. We derived a "creative thinking" measure by coding each diary narrative. A narrative was considered to have evidence of creative thinking if it described an event in which the person was engaged in any form of creative thinking as the term is used in everyday language; this included mentions of discovery, brainstorming, generating ideas, thinking flexibly, or "being creative." We also included many of the cognitive processes that theorists believe are important in facilitating creative thinking: learning, insight, realization, awareness, clarification, remembering, and focused concentration. All of these processes are included in what we call "creative thinking," "thinking creatively," or "creativity" in this article. (For more details on the methods and findings of our research, see the working paper by Teresa M. Amabile, Jennifer M. Mueller, William B. Simpson, Constance N. Hadley, Steven J. Kramer, and Lee Fleming, "Time Pressure and Creativity in Organizations: A Longitudinal Field Study," HBS, 2002.)

In preparing this article, we went beyond the statistical analyses of the time-pressure study to develop a richer view of the conditions under which time pressure may or may not have negative effects. For that purpose, we looked at four extreme conditions: days of very high time pressure when creative thinking did happen; days of very high time pressure when creative thinking didn't happen; days of very low time pressure when creative thinking did happen; and days of very low time pressure when creative thinking didn't happen. We took a sample of 100 diary entries from each of these four work conditions and read them carefully to discern patterns that distinguished them from one another—for instance, that creativity seemed more likely when people were able to focus on a single activity for most of the day.

In addition to that qualitative analysis, we used the numerical ratings that the participants reported in the questionnaires to examine the number of hours they worked; the degree of challenge, involvement, and time pressure they felt; the number of people they worked with; and the degree of distraction they felt. The results of our analyses are summarized in the exhibit "The Time-Pressure/Creativity Matrix."

A Peek into the Diaries

THESE DIARY EXCERPTS WERE written by study participants who experienced the four work conditions
described in this article. See if you or your employees
might say something similar about experiences in your
own organization.

On a Mission
(High Time Pressure,
High Likelihood
of Creative Thinking)

"At the end of the day today, after getting the documents ready, it hit me as to how creative Katherine and
I had been together when we had worked in a room,
away from the telephones, noise, interruptions, and
other distractions. I felt very satisfied with the work we
produced."

"Just as I was knee-deep in 1s and 0s, staring at an
execution trace of the firmware (which was acting
strangely),I got three phone calls in a row. I was about
ready to throw the damn phone across the room. Fortunately, it stopped ringing after that, and I was able to
refocus and find the problem. Hooray."

"We found out today that the drop test on one of our
products was not done properly, and we needed a way
to pad our product in a rush. I remembered that we had
$10 million worth of an obsolete cell cushion that we
were getting ready to write off, and I suggested we use
that. It worked great!"

"I brought in some of my personal camera equipment
today and used it to create a high-magnification video
analysis system . . . I felt this was very creative work on

my part—passing on my knowledge of optics and photography to an engineer who will continue with this work."

On an Expedition
(Low Time Pressure,
High Likelihood
of Creative Thinking)

"In my meeting with Seth to discuss the imaging model, several ideas he mentioned meshed with ideas I had, and I came away with a better and more detailed model."

"Wendy brought in her samples of the ILP films and presented them to me in a way that really made sense and triggered a lot of good ideas on my end."

"John spent time discussing promotional opportunities with me, and I felt like I was really learning something."

"I tried out my patterned adhesive wine labels in the lab. Bought wine at the grocery store and committed sacrilege by pouring it into the sink. My patterned adhesive didn't really work well, but I made some interesting observations that helped me understand the problem a little better."

"While brainstorming ideas for solving the axle retention problem, I discovered a way to reduce the cost of our current wheeled container. In addition, this may give us a better product that is easier to produce. I made a few calls to begin investigating the feasibility."

On a Treadmill
(High Time Pressure,
Low Likelihood
of Creative Thinking)

"I spent the day trying to get a business plan finished—or at least started—for this strategic alliance. I was very frustrated by constant interruptions, which make it necessary to get this type of work done before or after hours."

"Today was a very long day spent in several meetings. We spend so much time covering old issues instead of driving the business forward."

"I was informed that I have to come up with a new launch rationale by Monday so it can be reviewed by the operating team. The relaunching of the old printers is devoid of any logical strategy. Now I have to make up one that sounds good."

"One problem after another occurred today. I had intended to complete several different items for the product transfer, but I spent the day fighting fires instead."

On Autopilot
(Low Time Pressure,
Low Likelihood
of Creative Thinking)

"Very low energy today. Must be the weather, but I feel whipped. Focused on organizing and planning. Put out an agenda for the optimization meeting tomorrow."

"Overall feeling of depression today."

"Mostly just doing paperwork. I cleaned up a lot of outstanding items."

"The team had an all-day meeting with the general manager. He just raised three questions, rather than giving us a clear leadership response to what we've done."

"Today I gave a two-hour presentation on product strategy and plans for the new product launch to our European marketing managers. I was disappointed by their [apathetic] response. The same old issues came up and a moderately negative attitude prevailed."

Originally published in August 2002
Reprint R0208C

Tough-Minded Ways to Get Innovative

ANDRALL E. PEARSON

Executive Summary

CONSISTENT INNOVATION IS THE KEY to market leadership. Outstanding companies know that and build their success on it. And other organizations can do the same, the author explains in the HBR article from 1988, by making a systematic effort to concentrate on five key activities.

Start at the top. Innovation begins with a CEO or general manager who believes change is the way to survive. Spread that mind-set through the organization by setting challenging, measurable goals; getting everyone focused on beating a specific competitor; and supporting individuals who take risks.

Allow innovation to rise. The people and systems that run your business can choke off innovation. New ideas need champions, sponsors, a mix of creative types (for ideas) and operators (to keep things practical), and separate systems to get ideas to top management early and quickly.

Know the competitive dynamics of your business cold. A realistic strategic vision will channel innovative efforts to ideas that will pay off in the marketplace.

Determine where innovation lives. Look hard at your customers to find new segments, at your competitors to see what's already working, and at your own business to determine where you can leverage existing strengths.

Once an idea is well developed, go for broke. Expect heavy retaliation from competitors. Set priorities. Think through every step of the launch.

Although these steps sound simple enough to follow, innovation is a challenge from beginning to end. But it builds market leadership and competitive edge, which makes taking on the challenge worthwhile.

Like John Seely Brown, Andrall Pearson takes a broad view of innovation. And like Peter Drucker, he believes that productive innovation—the kind that actually makes a company more competitive—arises from discipline more than imagination. Pearson, an experienced corporate executive, sees innovation from the trenches, not from the clouds.

In his article "Tough-Minded Ways to Get Innovative," Pearson downplays the need for great product or technological breakthroughs, instead encouraging executives to seek steady, small enhancements in all business functions. Achieving that goal requires management that is simultaneously hardheaded and open-minded. You have to be ruthless in ferreting out information about your business's existing innovation investments and in cutting off those

*that don't have a clear strategic purpose. But you must
also have the guts to encourage your people to constantly
question their assumptions and to think freely about the
future. And when they do come up with a strategically
sound idea, you need to give them the resources they need
to bring it to fruition. When it comes to innovation, half
measures just don't cut it.*

MOST CHIEF EXECUTIVES FERVENTLY want their
companies to be more competitive, not just on one or
two dimensions but across the board. Yet outstanding
competitive performance remains an elusive goal. A few
companies achieve it. Most do not.

What distinguishes the outstanding competitors from
the rest? Two basic principles. First, they understand
that consistent innovation is the key to a company's survival. Being innovative some of the time, in one or two
areas, just won't work. Second, they know that the most
powerful changes they can make are those that create
value for their customers and potential customers. The
result? Competitive companies constantly look for ways
to change every aspect of their businesses. Then, when
they've found them, they make sure that they translate
those changes into advantages customers will appreciate
and act on.

Lincoln Electric has understood and applied these
principles for years. That's why it has been able to offer
its customers better products at lower cost year after
year. Yet many people see only Lincoln's success in cutting costs. They miss the fact that it is a great innovator
because they think about innovation too narrowly—in
terms of home runs only and not all the hits players
make, inning after inning, game after game.

Lincoln Electric and other outstanding performers look at innovation systematically. They know that their competitive successes are built on a steady stream of improvements in production, finance, distribution, and every other function, not just a big hit in sales or marketing or R&D. So they make sure they've got players who can deliver consistently. And they create organizations that give those players all the backup they need. That means

- creating and sustaining a corporate environment that values better performance above everything else,

- structuring the organization to permit innovative ideas to rise above the demands of running the business,

- clearly defining a strategic focus that lets the company channel its innovative efforts realistically—in ways that will pay off in the market,

- knowing where to look for good ideas and how to leverage them once they're found,

- going after good ideas at full speed, with all the company's resources brought to bear.

Individually, none of these activities may be very complicated or hard to do. But keeping a company focused on all five, all the time, takes tremendous discipline and persistence. That systematic effort to institutionalize innovation is what gives market leaders their edge. And it's what other companies can learn from them.

Begin with the Right Mind-Set

To convert a solid performer into an aggressive competitor, you have to create an organization that not only values better performance but also sustains the commitment year after year. That means a major shift in values, not a slight step-up in the number of new ideas for next year.

Even a brief exposure to companies that are consistently successful innovators shows their constant dedication to changing things for the better. Everyone in the business thinks and acts that way, not just a few people at the top. Just picture what it was like to work at Apple Computer or Cray Research or Nike in their early years. Or consider the way things are today at innovative leaders like Wal-Mart Stores or Toys "R" Us or Progressive Mutual Insurance. Or ask anyone at Heinz about the pressure on innovation since Tony O'Reilly introduced risk taking into that once sleepy outfit. Change is a way of life in companies like these.

To sharpen an organization's receptivity to change, several ingredients are essential. First and foremost, top management must be deeply and personally involved in the process.

Innovative companies are led by innovative leaders. It's that simple. Leaders who set demanding goals for themselves and for others, the kinds of goals that force organizations to innovate to meet them. Specific, measurable goals that constitute outstanding relative performance—like becoming number one in a particular market. Not vague, easily reached objectives.

Innovative leaders aren't necessarily creative, idea-driven people (though obviously many are). But they welcome change because they're convinced that their competitive survival depends on innovation. That's a mind-set most executives can develop—if their conviction is based on a specific understanding of a particular competitive environment, not just a bromidic generality.

Look at what Cummins Engine has done to stay alive and gain market share in a truck engine market that's dramatically off. As any key Cummins executive will tell you, the company cut its costs and prices per engine by close to 40% and materially improved its products for one simple reason: to prevent the Japanese from repeating their auto triumph in the truck engine business. To accomplish all this, Cummins had to overhaul nearly everything that, historically, had made it the industry leader: products, processes, prices, distribution methods—the works.

People throughout Cummins found the grit to make these changes by looking at their business through the eyes of a Japanese competitor. Other innovative companies do the same thing. They get their people to focus on beating a particular competitor, not just on doing better. One-on-one competition pushes the entire organization to be bolder, to take more risks, and to change more quickly than companies that have no particular target for their innovative efforts. It also makes a company a tighter, more effective competitor because its innovative efforts are designed to cut away at a particular opponent's current competitive advantages.

For instance, in the 1960s and early 1970s, PepsiCo was a much more aggressive and innovative company than Coca-Cola. It had to outflank Coke to survive. When Coke finally woke up—after losing its market leadership—it did a terrific job of innovating, too. Why? Coke's new management began to focus on beating Pepsi, not just on doing better. And when Pepsi's managers responded by revving up their already aggressive culture, the result made history. There has been more innovation in soft drinks in the past five years than there had been in the previous 20. Industry growth has doubled, and both companies' market shares are the highest ever.

The same thing happened in the beer business when Miller began to take market share from Anheuser-Busch. Suddenly Busch became a much more aggressive, innovative competitor because it was focused on Miller. In contrast, I believe IBM paid a huge price in the 1970s and early 1980s because the company wasn't focused on a number of specialized competitors that were eroding its leadership, segment by segment.

If you don't have any major competitors, you can't focus on them, of course. But targeting smaller local competitors is just as effective and invigorating. It's also a good way to ward off the complacency that undoes a lot of winners. At one time, for example, Frito-Lay thought that it didn't have to pay attention to its regional competitors since its market share was more than 50%. Then, collectively, the little guys cut the company's growth rate in half. Frito became very focused very fast.

Finally, innovative companies have lots of experiments going on all the time. This encourages more risk taking since people don't expect every experiment to succeed. It contains costs since tests and trials don't get expanded until they show real promise. And it improves the odds of success because you're betting on a portfolio, not on one or two big, long-odds projects.

Sometimes, however, the work environment is so risk averse that management has to bring in outsiders who haven't been intimidated by the sins of the past. That was what happened when PepsiCo acquired Taco Bell, which had been run by an ultraconservative management team that regarded all new ideas with suspicion. It took an infusion of three or four outsiders to create a critical mass and get the company moving again.

Unfortunately, it's very easy for managers to convey the wrong messages about risk taking. Appearing to be short-term oriented, giving the impression that only winners get promoted, searching for people to blame, second-guessing managers who take risks (often before they even have time to work out the bugs)—actions like these send a much clearer signal than all the speeches about innovation a chief executive may make. We learned that at PepsiCo when we surveyed our middle managers and found out that many of them thought we were saying one thing and doing another. We had to correct signals and practices like these before the managers would credit what we said.

All three of these ingredients—commitment, a specific villain, and risk taking—are soft requirements. Not tangible things like structure and process. But just because they're soft doesn't mean they're unimportant. In fact, unless all three are in place, I question whether you'll ever emerge as a leader.

Unsettle the Organization

Most big organizations are designed mainly to operate the business: to get the work done, control performance, spot problems, and bring in this year's results. And for the most part, that's as it should be.

But the structures, processes, and people that keep things ticking smoothly can also cut off the generation of good ideas and can block their movement through the business system. Excessive layering, for example, kills ideas before senior managers ever consider them. Barriers fencing off R&D, marketing, production, and finance block up functional problems until it's too late for effective solutions. Elaborate approval systems grind promising innovations to a halt. Staffers nitpick ideas or put financial yardsticks on them long before they are mature enough to stand rigorous scrutiny.

To get around organizational roadblocks like these you have to differentiate between what's needed to run the business and what's needed to foster creative activity. Most successful innovations require four key inputs:

- a champion who believes that the new idea is really critical and who will keep pushing ahead, no matter what the roadblocks;

- a sponsor who is high up enough in the organization to marshal its resources—people, money, and time;

- a mix of bright, creative minds (to get ideas) and experienced operators (to keep things practical);

- a process that moves ideas through the system quickly so that they get top-level assessment, endorsement, and resources early in the game—not at the bottom of the ninth inning.

There are, of course, lots of ways to organize your company to bring these four elements together. One is to use task forces on either a full- or part-time basis. Even Procter & Gamble (the ultimate product-manager company) has begun to superimpose multifunctional project teams, often headed by senior managers, onto its old structure. Other companies use full-time task forces to achieve similar goals. They've found their old structures didn't allow enough cross-functional interaction early on. Or enough top-level involvement and support.

Still other companies, like Hasbro, rely on frequent, consistent, and freewheeling meetings with top management to achieve their integration goals. They work within the existing structure but install a process to prevent rigidity and delay. Johnson & Johnson, on the other hand, has thrived largely by spinning off operations into small divisions to encourage its general managers to act more like freestanding entrepreneurs. In all these cases, the companies are striving to create the freedom needed to cross lines, get a variety of inputs, and take risks. They've tried to organize the creative parts of the company differently from the operational ones.

These efforts aren't cost free, of course. When you're trying to change and run the business at the same time, there's bound to be some competition and conflict. But bright people can live with that, and sooner or later the bumps get smoothed out. The risk I'd worry about is leaving one of the critical bases uncovered—by trying to make a champion out of someone who isn't committed to a project, say, or neglecting to temper your whiz kids with some seasoned people who'll be able to tell them whether the product they envision can actually be made. Because if you announce you're going to innovate more aggressively, yet you consistently come up short, people will get discouraged and turn off.

Be Hardheaded About Your Strategy

Once the entire organization is committed to stepping up the pace of innovation, you have to decide where to direct your efforts. One way, of course, is to put smart and talented people to work and pray that they'll come up with something great. But more often than not, an unfocused approach like that produces lots of small ideas that don't lead anywhere, big costs and embarrassing write-offs, and a great deal of frustration and stop-and-go activity.

In contrast, successful innovators usually have a pretty clear idea of the kind of competitive edge they're seeking. They've thought long and hard about what's practical in their particular business. And just as hard about what's not.

Frequently, you'll hear CEOs say that their company is committed to becoming the low-cost producer, or the industry leader in new products and production processes, or the best service provider. All are worthy visions or concepts—provided they apply to that particular business and company. But in many cases, the vision and the reality don't match up.

For much of smokestack America, for example, the concept of becoming the low-cost producer is simply a cruel fantasy. The Japanese already occupy that position, in many cases permanently. So the best that U.S. manufacturers can possibly hope for is to close the gap, which isn't likely to bring them back to being number one.

Likewise, leading the way in new products has turned out to be a fool's mission for most companies in mature industries like packaged goods. The reason? Fewer than ten new products a year are successful, despite expenditures of literally tens of millions of dollars by the major companies.

Finally, superior service can be an illusory and impractical goal for many large retailers. It simply takes more management and discipline than they can muster to bring so many outlets up to a higher-than-average level of service and keep them there.

The moral here is that your strategic vision has to be grounded in a deep understanding of the competitive dynamics of your business. You have to know the industry and your competitors cold. You have to know how you stack up on every performance dimension (the way Ford did before it was able to close the gap on some 300 product features on which it lagged behind Japanese competitors). And you have to be hardheaded about using this knowledge to position your company to gain a competitive edge. Are you big enough? Technically strong enough? Good enough at marketing? In short, you must be practical—not go after a pie in the sky.

Hasbro, a $1.5 billion (and growing) toy company, has a strategic vision that works. Unlike most of its competitors, Hasbro doesn't focus on inventing new blockbuster toys. Its management will take blockbusters if they come along, of course. But the company doesn't spend the bulk of its product development dollars on such long-odds bets. Instead, it centers its efforts on staples—toy lines like G.I. Joe, Transformers, games, and preschool basics that can be extended and renewed each year.

Another fine example is Crown Cork & Seal, one of America's best-performing companies for more than 30 years despite its five-star terrible business—tin cans.

Good ideas most often flow from the process of taking a hard look at your customers, your competitors, and your business all at once.

How did Crown do it, especially when it was number four, dominated by two giants (American Can and Continental Can) that were in a mature business where size and scale appear to be essential? Simple. Crown focused its efforts on growth segments (beverages), on being the lowest-cost producer in each local area (instead of nationally), on growing in less-developed countries (too small for the biggies to worry about), and on taking over the profitable, residual business left open as Continental and American diversified out of cans.

Both Hasbro and Crown Cork & Seal are tightly focused; they don't try to be all things to all customers. And because their directions are so clearly set, their creative people can channel their efforts toward things that will work against competitors in their particular businesses. Strategic focus works—in real life, not just in articles about strategy.

Look Hard at What's Already Going On

How do you find good, concrete ideas? Brainstorming is one approach, but I've never found that very helpful, except when nobody in the group knows much and nobody cares whether the output is realistic. No, I firmly believe the best backdrop for spurring innovation is knowledge—knowing your business cold. Good ideas most often flow from the process of taking a hard look at your customers, your competitors, and your business all at once. So in looking for ways to innovate, I'd concentrate on

- what's already working in the marketplace that you can improve on as well as expand,

- how you can segment your markets differently and gain a competitive advantage in the process,

- how your business system compares with your competitors'.

Looking hard at what's already working in the marketplace is the tactic likely to produce the quickest results. I call this robbing a few gas stations so that you don't starve to death while you're planning the perfect crime.

Lots of companies think that the only good innovations are the ones they develop themselves, not the ideas they get from smaller competitors—the familiar not-invented-here syndrome. In my experience, the opposite is usually true. Normally, outside ideas are useful simply because your competitors are already doing your market research for you. They're proving what customers want in the marketplace, where it counts.

I've found that good ideas come from all over—conventional competitors, regionals, small companies, even international competitors in Europe and Japan. So it may not surprise you to learn that most of PepsiCo's major strategic successes are ideas we borrowed from the marketplace—often from small regional or local competitors.

For example, Doritos, Tostitos, and Sabritos (whose combined sales total roughly $1 billion) were products developed by three small chippers on the West Coast. The idea for pan pizza (a $500 million business for Kansas-based Pizza Hut) originated with several local pizzerias in Chicago. And the pattern for Wilson 1200 golf clubs (the most successful new club line ever) came from a small golf clubber in Arizona.

In each case, PepsiCo spotted a promising new idea, improved on it, and then outexecuted the competition. To some people this sounds like copycatting. To me it amounts to finding out what's working with consumers, improving on the concept, then getting more out of it. You can decide how much this idea appeals to you. But at PepsiCo it led to $2 billion to $3 billion worth of successful innovations. And without those innovations, the company's growth would have been a lot less dynamic.

Next, I'd look at how to create segments or markets for your products. It sounds simple, but, believe me, it takes a lot of creativity and skill to segment a market beyond simple demographics (which rarely ever produce meaningful segment edges or boundaries), ferret out what individual groups of consumers really want (as opposed to what they say they want), and actually create distinctive product performance features (despite the technological and operational problems you usually encounter).

Several examples illustrate what I have in mind. At Taco Bell, the biggest Mexican fast-food chain in the United States, top management found that working women were avoiding its outlets like the plague. Women felt Taco Bell's food was "too heavy," "too spicy." So the company developed a taco salad served in a light flour tortilla and seasoned very mildly. The addition of that salad increased per-store sales more than 20%, with 70% of the sales coming from women—mostly new customers. It also added about $100 million to Taco Bell's sales in its first full year.

It sounds simple, I'm sure: Pick out a big segment you're not reaching, find out what consumers don't like about existing products, and develop a product to serve them better. But it took Taco Bell nearly two years to get the idea, develop it in R&D, test-market several versions of the salad, and finally launch the winner nationally.

Another, much more familiar, example is what the Japanese have done in the camera business. They decided that a segment of camera users couldn't afford German top-of-the-line models but wanted vastly better pictures than they could take with their Kodaks or Polaroids. Camera technology has been around for a long time, and the Japanese just hammered away at improving it until they succeeded in making superior 35mm cameras at a price people could afford. In the process, they created and now dominate a huge segment that no one else had seen.

Finally, there's Budget Gourmet, a four-year-old company you may never have heard of. Its management developed a profitable $300 million business from scratch in a field—frozen foods—characterized by enormous price pressures, undistinguished products, little innovation, as well as low returns. The founder's strategic vision was to offer working families high-quality products intended for microwave ovens and aimed at the low end of the market.

So the company started out by developing a process to make and sell a line of entrées for $1.69 each, which gave it a good price advantage. But unlike other low-priced lines, Budget Gourmet's products were comparable to the over-$2 competition. And it backed up the product with first-class packaging, promotion, and advertising (the kind its low-end competitors didn't think of investing in).

The result—a remarkable success in an extremely competitive field previously dominated by three of America's largest, most successful food companies. It's a terrific example of how segmentation and strategic focus interact. And, like most good ideas, it looks obvious—once you see how it works.

As these examples show, successful segmenters are very clear about what they're trying to do: offer their customers better value than their competitors do. This usually takes one of three forms: lower prices, better-performing products, or better features for certain uses (a niche). Unless you can beat your competitors on one of these three dimensions, your innovation probably won't be a big success. The key idea, of course, is that you're trying to outperform the competition on a specific performance dimension and scale, not with vague platitudes. And successful innovators don't give up until customers reassure them that they've done just that.

The third place to look for good innovative ideas is in your business system. Beyond its products, every company has a business system by which it goes to market. That system is the whole flow of activities, starting with product design and working its way through purchasing, production, MIS, distribution, customer sales, and product service. It will come as no surprise that these systems differ from one competitor to another, even in the same industry. And in almost every case, each competitor's system has particular strengths and vulnerabilities that can provide a fruitful focus for your innovative energies.

The underlying concept here is that a distinctive system can give you a big competitive edge for all your products because it will help you leverage their inherent consumer appeal in ways your competitors find hard to match. And once you understand how your business's system works at each step—both in terms of the marketplace and comparative system costs—it's surprising how often you'll uncover weak spots in a competitor's system or potential strengths in your own.

The number of Pizza Hut outlets (4,500), for example, dwarfs that of its nearest competitor (about 500). Scale like that is no guarantee of success. But it means that only the Pizza Hut system can market pizza products on a national basis virtually overnight—and thereby preempt local competition.

At one time, the biggest marketing problem Pizza Hut faced was lunch. Compared with McDonald's, its restaurants had virtually no lunchtime sales, and neither did any of its pizza competitors. The reason, of course, is that it takes 20 minutes to cook a pizza from scratch in a traditional pizza oven, and most people won't spend that long at lunchtime waiting to be served. By using a new, continuous-broiling technology adapted from the burger business, Pizza Hut developed a personal pan pizza that could be served in less than five minutes. It was quick, tasty, and moderately priced. And Pizza Hut rolled it out to all 4,500 stores and locked up the pizza-lunch business almost everywhere, almost overnight.

Another good example of using a business system to maintain a competitive edge comes from the cookie business. P&G decided it could produce better cookies than Nabisco, the current leader, could. So the company came out with a great cookie that tasted and looked better than Nabisco's Chips Ahoy!, the market leader. Duncan Hines cookies were the kind of superior product P&G has used to become the market leader time and time again.

But its managers didn't count on the retaliatory strength of Nabisco's direct store-to-door distribution system and its intense desire to protect that big, profitable base system.

Nabisco quickly matched P&G's cookie, in addition to expanding and improving its entire cookie line. Nabisco also used the leverage of its bigger system to get trade support and consumer impact. Despite the inherent superiority of P&G's single-product entry, it stood no chance against Nabisco's system strengths.

Virtually any part of your business system can be the basis for building a competitive edge. Product technology has been a fruitful source of systemic advantage for Cray Research. Lincoln Electric's decades-long leadership is based largely on a systemic edge in production. Truly superior marketing and service have made Fidelity Investments' Fidelity Funds the dominant player in a business where it was once an also-ran.

Even the best concepts or strategies tend to develop incrementally. They rarely ever work the first time out or unfold just as they were planned.

Naturally, in analyzing your business system and your competitors', you have to look at them dynamically since structural changes are usually at work altering what's required for success. When Philip Morris bought 7-Up, for example, its management knew the company was entering an industry that historically had allowed smaller brands to prosper nicely. In fact, many Coke and Pepsi bottlers also handled 7-Up. But the battle between Coke and Pepsi was heating up, and as it intensified, those cola competitors put tremendous pressure on their bottlers to launch new products, promote more often, and scramble for supermarket space. Both 7-Up and its new cola brand were left out in the cold. A once forgiving industry had become downright hostile.

Go for Broke

Even the best concepts or strategies tend to develop incrementally. They rarely ever work the first time out or unfold just as they were planned. In fact, the original concept or its execution usually gets changed considerably before it's ready to be implemented broadly. Pizza Hut's pan pizza, for instance, went through four or five iterations. So even after you spot a promising segment and develop a product to serve it, you've usually still got at least one major hurdle to jump before you can capitalize on your new idea.

Tab initially flopped as a diet cola because consumers couldn't tell the difference between Tab with one calorie and Diet Pepsi, which then had 100. Then Coke figured out that it could dramatize the difference by surrounding a bathing beauty with 100 empty Tab bottles. Armed with that insight, Coke flooded the TV screen with ads and backed them up in stores with displays, signs, and samples. It was frightening to see how quickly that one idea, which sounds pretty small, changed the competitive dynamics.

To take another example, the Wilson Sting graphite tennis racket was developed to sell for half the price of

the Prince graphite racket. But very few high-end consumers believed they could get the same quality racket
for $125 as Prince provided for $250, even though the less
expensive racket was indeed as good a product as the
more costly one. Fortunately, an alert marketing person
at Wilson then uncovered a new segment for the Sting—
people who were buying metal rackets because they
couldn't afford graphite. Sting's pitch became "a graphite
racket for the same price as steel," and that positioning
made it a major success.

Once an idea or a concept is properly developed, it
seems logical to assume that any sensible company
would throw the book at it to make it a success. Yet I've
found that reality is often quite different. As I look back,
most of the new-product mistakes I've seen grew from a
company's failure to back up the innovation with enough
resources—not from overspending.

Several factors explain this phenomenon. First and
most important, many people fail to recognize that their
competitors will retaliate—especially if their innovation
takes customers away. People get so captivated by their
own product that they plan launches implicitly assuming
there will be no significant competitive response. Almost
inevitably, that turns out to be a poor assumption.

Second, people try to stretch their resources to
finance too many projects at once because the prospect
of four or five successes instead of one or two is so
attractive. But new products generally involve considerable front-end investment and lots of management
attention. So in a world where money, people, and programs are necessarily limited, this usually means that
none of the projects get enough sustained support and
effort to be guaranteed success. The only way around it is
to be disciplined enough to say "next year" to most of the
good ideas available.

Finally, people are often in such a hurry to get a new product to market that they neglect to think through all the things needed to launch it properly. These include programs to get adequate retailer support, advertising to generate high customer awareness, and above all, trial-inducing devices to entice consumers to pick the new product instead of the one they're already using. One or more of these essentials often go by the boards.

In contrast, the big winners make careful plans to throw everything needed at new products to ensure their success—money, people, programs in every functional area. They don't just allocate resources; they marshal them, and then they execute them like the Russian hockey team or the Boston Celtics. The successful companies have learned that doing it right the first time is lots more effective (and usually far less costly) than doing the job on a shoestring and then scrambling to fix things when what happens doesn't meet expectations. They also know they're never going to have the first-blood advantage again, and that the best way to preempt or block out competition is to do it right the first time.

I'm a firm believer in developing innovations as fast as you can do each one properly, which includes stopping to be sure you've got everything needed to generate a big success and then going to war to make the idea a winner. It sounds so obvious, you wonder why so many companies fail to execute either of these pieces properly.

To sum up quickly, I believe there are five steps you can take to make your company more dynamic and innovative: Create a corporate environment that puts constant pressure on everyone to beat your specific competitors at innovation. Structure your organization so that you promote innovation instead of thwarting it. Develop a realistic strategic focus to channel your innovative efforts. Know where to look for good ideas and how to use your business system to leverage them once they're found. Throw the book at good ideas once you've developed them fully.

It all sounds simple because, of course, it is. Simple but not easy, since each innovation is a constant challenge from beginning to end. Yet innovation is a challenge you have to meet because that's what builds market leadership and competitive momentum. That's the bottom line. And that's why it's worth the extra effort to become an innovative company.

Originally published in August 2002
Reprint R0208H

Breaking Out of the Innovation Box

JOHN D. WOLPERT

Executive Summary

IN MOST COMPANIES, investments in innovation follow a boom-bust cycle. For a time, the cash flows. Then, as the economy sours or companies rethink their priorities, the taps go dry.

But when research budgets are slashed, the strong projects are often abandoned along with the weak ones. Promising initiatives are cut off just when they are about to bear fruit. Expensive labs are closed; partnership agreements costing millions in legal fees are thrown away. When disruptive changes in the competitive landscape come, companies are caught flat-footed.

Sustainable innovation requires a new approach: Instead of being largely isolated projects, innovation initiatives need to gain access to the insights and capabilities of other companies. To be protected from the ax of short-term cost reductions and the faddishness born of easy money, the initiatives must become part of the ongoing commerce that takes place among companies.

But how can businesses traffic in such sensitive information without giving their competitors an advantage?

The answer, the author contends, lies in a practice that's been common since the Middle Ages: the use of independent intermediaries to facilitate the exchange of sensitive information among companies without revealing the principals' identities or motives and without otherwise compromising their interests. Executive search firms, for example, allow job seekers to remain anonymous during the early stages of a search, and they protect businesses from disclosing their hiring plans to rivals.

A network of innovation intermediaries would be in a unique position to visualize new opportunities synthesized from insights and technologies provided by several companies—ideas that might never occur to businesses working on their own.

As THE ECONOMY BOOMED in the late 1990s, corporations went on an innovation binge. They poured money into programs for generating fresh ideas, pioneering new technologies, and promoting entrepreneurship and creativity among employees. They launched venture capital arms and new-business incubators. They recruited freethinking executives who weren't afraid to rock the corporate boat. They brought in creativity consultants to spur out-of-the-box thinking.

And where are those efforts today? Many of them have been scaled back, mothballed, or disbanded altogether. As the economy cooled at the start of this decade, companies quickly cut off the flow of funds into innovation efforts. What seemed like a mandatory expense just months before suddenly seemed discretionary. Even the rhetoric of business took a turn: Executives began to speak less about "creating the future" and more about "protecting the core."

What happened over the last few years is not an anomaly. It's business as usual. In most companies, investments in innovation follow a boom-bust cycle. For a time, the cash flows. Then, as companies rethink their priorities, the taps go dry. Annual surveys conducted by the Industrial Research Institute confirm the cyclicality of corporate innovation. In the early 1980s, surveyed executives said that innovation was their foremost priority. By the late 1980s, most executives reported little interest in innovation. Similarly, in the early 1990s, innovation didn't rate among the top five corporate priorities, but it was back at the top of the list by the late 1990s. Harvard Business School professor Henry Chesbrough has identified a similar pattern in the 1960s.

Of course, no business initiative should be immune to changes in market conditions or company strategies. Corporate innovation programs should be subject to careful, hard-nosed evaluation, and those that don't promise adequate returns should be curtailed or refocused. But that is not what is going on here. Rather, the way corporations invest in innovation is fundamentally unreliable. When innovation budgets are slashed, strong projects are abandoned along with the weak. The consequences can be devastating. Promising initiatives are cut off just when they are about to bear fruit. Highly touted training programs are discontinued with little explanation, stirring employee cynicism. Expensive labs are closed, and talented researchers and designers are reassigned or laid off. Partnership agreements costing millions in legal fees are thrown away. Worst of all, the perceived failure of the investments often creates organizational skepticism about and resistance to future innovation initiatives. Consequently, when disruptive changes in the competitive landscape come, companies are caught flat-footed.

Innovation is always a risky pursuit, with an uncertain and often distant payoff. But must that fact doom it to erratic investment? Or can innovation become a staple corporate priority as, for example, quality has become? My belief is that stability can be brought to corporate innovation and that the result will be much greater strategic gains and much stronger returns on investment. But sustainable innovation requires an entirely new approach. Instead of being a largely isolated process— carried out often with considerable secrecy—innovation needs to become more open. Initiatives must gain access to and leverage from the insights, capabilities, and support of other companies without compromising legitimate corporate secrets. As counterintuitive as this may sound, innovation must become part of the ongoing commerce that takes place among companies. Only then will it be protected from both the ax of short-term cost reduction and the faddishness born of easy money.

Trapped Inside

First, let me explain what I mean by "innovation." I'm not talking about processes for making improvements to existing products and services. And I'm not talking about purely technical invention. Innovation, as I use the term, means pursuing radical new business opportunities, exploiting new or potentially disruptive technologies, and introducing change into the core concept of your business. It's those efforts that businesses have found hard to sustain, even though it is now widely acknowledged that they have become increasingly critical to companies' long-term viability. In fact, nearly 50% of U.S. economic growth at the end of the 1990s came from lines of business that didn't exist a decade before, as a 1999 study in *The Economist* showed.

Successful innovation requires what the authors of *Radical Innovation* have called "exploration competencies"—the ability to harvest ideas and expertise from a wide array of sources.[1] For a company, that means bringing in insights and know-how not just from outside parties but from other businesses. The need for external perspectives seems almost self-evident: If a company stays locked inside its own four walls, how will it be able to uncover and exploit opportunities outside its existing businesses or beyond its current technical or operational capabilities? Yet perhaps even more self-evident to many companies is the need to lock in their innovation initiatives to protect them from competitors.

This urge to keep innovation inside is reinforced by both traditional and current thinking on the subject. If you look at the examples of innovation cited in books and articles, you'll find that almost all of them describe the exploits of a group of employees within a single company—how they stumble on a new opportunity, struggle to overcome company politics and other internal impediments, and ultimately either succeed or fail to commercialize their discovery. Most theories of innovation are similarly introspective. Gifford Pinchot III coined the term "intrapreneuring" in the 1970s; the very name implies an internal focus. Rensselaer Polytechnic's Severino Center for Technological Entrepreneurship recommends building internal innovation hubs. Many management gurus suggest that innovation be thought of as a core competency—a distinctive capability that a company nurtures within itself and protects from outside competitors. Even the concept of "knowledge brokering," which sounds like it should involve collaboration between companies and across industries, is most often described in terms of individuals and groups working within one company.

But organizing innovation as a purely internal initiative pretty much guarantees that cyclical pressures will lead executives to cut back or discontinue funding. No matter how loudly a CEO proclaims the need to embed innovation and creativity in the corporate culture, the fact is that such initiatives are cut when times get tough or priorities change.

Typical is the experience of a large telecom company's ill-fated innovation program, which was called the Opportunity Discovery Department (ODD). Launched in 1995, its mission was to uncover promising ideas in the company, spread insights and expertise across the organization, and translate technologies from R&D labs into commercial opportunities. The ODD team received generous funding and considerable management support. Lab directors, and even the CEO himself, repeatedly encouraged managers and employees to collaborate with the group. Nevertheless, the team lost momentum. By 1999, the ODD had ceased operations.

No company is smart enough to know what to do with every new opportunity it finds, and no company has enough resources to pursue all the opportunities it might execute.

Many internal innovation initiatives have shared the ODD's fate. They last, on average, about three or four years. In most cases, that is not enough time to discover strong new business ideas and refine, test, launch, and nurture them to success. A study of innovation at Xerox that Chesbrough did showed that over a 35-year period its most successful spin-offs took an average of 7.5 years to generate an acceptable return on investment. That didn't include the time spent researching and developing the underlying technologies. However, the innovation programs that generated those spin-offs survived an average of only four years before they were shut down and replaced by new ones. Often, those initiatives were terminated even though the spin-offs they had generated had notched up substantial financial returns. As one Xerox executive explains: "We are a $20 billion company. To be financially interesting to us, an initiative must reach at least $100 million in revenues within three years." That argument, which will sound familiar to many executives, explains why large companies fail to sustain even lucrative innovation programs.

There's another problem with inward-looking innovation initiatives: They often fail to capitalize on viable ideas because the ideas don't fit with the company's strategy or capabilities. No company is smart enough to know what to do with every new opportunity it finds, and no company has enough resources to pursue all the opportunities it might execute. Internal initiatives routinely leave a trail of orphans—promising ideas that have no natural home within the company. If the number of orphans produced becomes too large relative to the successes—and it almost always does at large companies—participants' interest in the initiative falls.

Spinning out orphans as separate entities is possible but, despite the hype surrounding spin-offs, it rarely happens. Few companies have the patience or skills to do them well and, in any case, companies routinely kill

spin-off proposals because they fear losing the intellectual property to outsiders. In the past, some orphans
escaped corporate labs, falling into the hands of others
both eager and able to capitalize on them. In the information technology business, for example, breakthrough
technologies like Ethernet, the mouse, and the graphical
user interface were commercialized by companies that
did not develop them. But with aggressive patenting
practices, that will happen much less frequently in the
future. As Bell Labs' new-ventures chief, Thomas
Uhlman, famously said in 1999, "No more Intels are
allowed to escape." Unfortunately, that means that as
long as innovation is trapped inside individual companies, many promising technologies and business ideas
will simply die without ever being exploited.

Innovation as Commerce

No company is, of course, hermetically sealed. Outside
perspectives and competencies flow into and out of organizations through many routes: partnerships with universities, alliances and acquisitions, external venture
investments, recruiting and hiring, customers and suppliers, and the relationships and curiosity of individual
employees. These sources of external influence are valuable and important. It could be argued, in fact, that they
have played pivotal roles in all instances of corporate
innovation.

But they're not enough. Their informality, haphazard-
ness, and unpredictability make them unreliable founda-
tions for sustained innovation. New hires, for instance,
may come into a company with brilliant, radical ideas,
but they usually find it difficult if not impossible to promote those ideas in an alien, and often resistant, culture.

Academic cooperation usually centers on basic science—
one might argue that looking for new business ideas in
academia is like fishing for marlin in a trout stream. Customers and suppliers, as Harvard Business School's Clay-
ton Christensen has shown, tend to provide limited
insight beyond incremental improvements to existing
lines. Even more formal means for capitalizing on external business ideas, from venture capital arms to joint
ventures to M&A programs, are rarely dependable as
sources of innovation. They tend to be so determinis-
tic—so shaped by internal strategies, politics, and
secrecy concerns—that they perpetuate a company's
existing businesses rather than open new opportunities.
Moreover, the search for outside partners often happens
late in the innovation process, when the business opportunity is well defined, so they have little or no influence
over the development and refinement of the idea. Successful innovation depends on involving partners early in
the exploration of opportunities.

What we need to do is make innovation a natural element of the commerce that takes place among businesses. Finding ways for two or more companies to
actively share ideas, technologies, and other capabilities
early and often is the best way to protect projects from
the swings in interest and funding that inevitably occur
in individual organizations. If we could find a way to do
this without risking the unauthorized appropriation of
intellectual property, businesses would be able to more
quickly spot and exploit new growth opportunities.

In an ideal world, where there is no fear of competitors, here's how it would work: If company A develops a
great idea that it can't commercialize, it can more efficiently shift it to company B, which has the right skills,
particularly if the two businesses strike a relationship at

a very early stage of idea development. If company C lacks two particular capabilities needed to bring a technology to market, it can form a partnership with companies D and E to gain the required resources. If companies F, G, and H share a common interest in a certain business opportunity but lack the cash or strategic focus to pursue it independently, they can pool their investments. When innovation becomes part of commerce, money and attention flow naturally to where they're needed when they're needed.

The case of IBM's alphaWorks, which I oversaw for two years in the late 1990s, shows the power of open innovation. In early 1996, IBM's Internet Division realized that the company had developed many promising software programs in research that had yet to be commercialized. As an experiment, the division created a public Web site called alphaWorks on which it posted the programs, hoping that outside companies and developers would contribute valuable ideas about bringing them to market. Anyone could download the programs with a 90-day evaluation license from the company. As word spread that IBM was allowing first-cut versions of its research technology to be used for free, hundreds of thousands of early adopters, innovators, and entrepreneurs came to the site to download the software. Many of these users were technically savvy developers and businesspeople who had the skills to see the opportunities in that raw code.

One IBM researcher, who had been trying for years to find a compelling use for his program, received ideas from a developer at another company through alphaWorks. That helped him take his research in a new direction, eventually leading to the development of a critical component for the multibillion-dollar business integration-systems market. When thousands of people began to download that program, an IBM product group quickly decided to develop and release a full-fledged version. Within eight weeks, the once-ignored program had become a key IBM product. Without this kind of early external support, the researcher's work might still be waiting to go to market today.

Launched six years ago, alphaWorks is still a staple of IBM's innovation agenda. Its productivity is high: About 40% of the technologies on the site make it to market as new offerings, new features in existing products, or new technical standards. Unlike other innovative programs that die after the original champion leaves, the group has survived several management changes and divisional reorganizations. Indeed, it would be hard to kill alpha-Works because so many people in IBM rely on it to do their jobs, and nobody would want to sever connections to this large, influential, and involved community. It remains the best way for many of IBM's engineers to get recognition, feedback, and support for their ideas. It also has the attention of IBM's marketing people, who were initially stunned to find current and potential customers asking them when alphaWorks technologies would become commercially available. Most of IBM's strategic software initiatives since 1996 have started on alpha-Works.

Why don't competitors simply help themselves to these ideas? For one thing, patents and licenses are easy to enforce. Putting the ideas on a popular Web site (often with significant press coverage) means that everyone knows where they came from. Thanks to download logs and registration, anyone foolish enough to download a technology and then try to bring something similar to market would be caught red-handed in violation of the license and the patent.

IBM's alphaWorks—and similar initiatives like Xerox's new alphaAvenue—have limited applicability, of course. Not every business innovation benefits from public exposure as much as software development does. But they clearly show how a successful innovation marketplace that crosses the border of the firm perpetuates itself, gaining increasing attention and support as it delivers real economic benefits to many different participants inside and outside the company. The broader question is: How do you break down the barriers to sharing information across companies so you can create more generalized sustainable innovation markets without giving your competitors an advantage?

A New Kind of Go-Between

The answer, I believe, lies in a practice that has long been a central element in commerce: the use of independent intermediaries to facilitate the exchange of sensitive information among companies. Since the Middle Ages, businesspeople have drawn on trusted middlemen to share confidential information without revealing the principals' identities or motives or otherwise compromising their interests. Today, businesses continue to use intermediaries for many kinds of transactions. Executive search firms, for instance, play a crucial role in recruiting top managers. They allow job seekers to remain anonymous during the early stages of a search, and they protect businesses from disclosing their hiring plans to rivals.

In a similar way, intermediaries could facilitate the exchange of innovation information while protecting companies from divulging their interests and plans to competitors. They could become, in effect, innovation headhunters. A company might, to take a simple example, entrust an intermediary with the details of a particular technology it has developed as well as its need for outside capabilities to commercialize it. The intermediary would then share the information with other intermediaries in the hope of finding appropriate partners. At no point—until a formal disclosure agreement is forged—would any of the information be shared with the companies the intermediaries represent. The intermediaries could be trusted to maintain confidentiality because it is simply in their business interest: If they ever violate the terms of an arrangement, no company would hire them again.

Using intermediaries for innovation is not without precedent in U.S. business. In their book *Information Markets: What Businesses Can Learn from Financial Innovation*, William J. Wilhelm, Jr., and Joseph D. Downing describe how intermediaries spurred innovation in financial services in the early part of the twentieth century. The intermediaries, including bankers such as J.P. Morgan, assisted in creating markets for financial information. They used personal relationships to gather and share information discreetly with people in their network who could help exploit a new opportunity or a new way of handling financial transactions. "Innovation flourished," the authors write, "in the context of close relationships and powerful intermediaries that tempered competition but protected easily copied ideas and products. This protection encouraged financial innovation by more nearly ensuring a fair return on investment in intellectual property."

Even today, a number of individuals and organizations play intermediary roles in facilitating innovation. Management consultancies like Accenture and Cap Gemini Ernst & Young operate innovation labs, where clients can share ideas and discuss technological advances and other new research. Ideo, the design firm, often creates new products by mixing together the ideas and technologies of different clients. As a business development consultancy, ISIS International has for more than 20 years acted as an intermediary to cross-fertilize business opportunities for its clients.

ISIS, for example, recently helped the chemical division of a major U.S. oil company find commercial applications for a new molecule it had developed. Although the molecule seemed promising, its potential applications were not immediately obvious to the division's R&D staff. They hired ISIS to search outside the company for possibilities.

Perhaps the most promising pool of potential intermediaries is the rapidly growing population of baby boomer retirees.

ISIS convened a brainstorming summit with 12 of its contacts in industries ranging from waste treatment and building materials to cosmetics and household-cleaning products. The panel quickly identified 11 business opportunities for the molecule, with potential revenues of $150 million. One of the companies represented on the panel went on to pursue a joint project with the oil company and introduced a new consumer product based on the molecule. Without the catalytic role ISIS played, the project may have been killed before it had the chance to be successful.

Unfortunately, most consulting firms consider sharing perspectives and competencies among clients to be taboo. Consultants, therefore, are unlikely to be a major source of innovation intermediaries. But there are plenty of other players operating in and around the innovation process who could function as intermediaries. Lawyers and venture capitalists, for instance, often learn about best practices, ideas for new inventions, and new ways of doing business from competing and noncompeting companies. Trade show organizers and trade association representatives frequently conduct high-level meetings between potential buyers, suppliers, and partners, and identify opportunities for synergy within and across industries. Investment bankers are often called upon to find new applications for technologies developed by companies or government agencies.

But perhaps the most promising pool of potential intermediaries is the rapidly growing population of baby boomer retirees who have deep expertise in particular industries and technologies, hold the trust of the companies they worked for, and don't want to spend all their time playing golf. With the right training in such disciplines as knowledge brokering, business development, and law, these former corporate executives, scientists, and engineers would make ideal agents. And by using the Internet to communicate and share information with their clients and one another, they could position themselves in the idea flow without abandoning their other retirement pursuits.

Sitting at the intersection of many companies and industries, a network of innovation intermediaries would be in a unique position to visualize new opportunities.

Ultimately, I believe we will see the emergence of formal networks, perhaps even companies of such agents. Businesses would pay an annual fee to hire a group of intermediaries with the appropriate backgrounds and contacts, briefing them about their internal innovation programs. Bound by nondisclosure agreements, the agents would share information with other agents representing other companies. The agents would signal their clients when they thought sharing data would be worthwhile, and they would help structure the terms of the engagement. Whenever it was mutually beneficial, intercompany innovation relationships would form early and often through this relatively safe, controlled network. Sitting at the intersection of many companies and industries, a network of innovation intermediaries would be in a unique position to visualize new opportunities synthesized from insights and technologies provided by several companies—ideas that might never occur to companies working on innovation programs on their own. (See "A Network of Intermediaries" at the end of this article).

The final shape of such intermediation networks is impossible to predict. In fact, other means of collaboration may develop. We may, for instance, see the emergence of new Web services that automate some of the basic information exchange essential to creative partnerships. Or we may see companies offer data-mining services that generate new business ideas by analyzing information collected from several companies at once without violating privacy or exposing secrets. What's certain is that, in an increasingly complex world, the biggest growth opportunities will come more often at the intersection of multiple companies than from single visionaries acting on their own. It's important now that companies break out of their innovation boxes and find ways to link their innovation efforts. In the years ahead, the greatest corporate innovation may arise in the innovation process itself.

A Network of Intermediaries

INTERMEDIARIES COULD FACILITATE the exchange of information about innovation among companies while keeping their secrets. If company A, for instance, needs outside capabilities to commercialize a technology, it could ask its intermediary to find it a partner. The intermediary would share the information with other intermediaries in its search for an appropriate collaborator—like company B. In the same way, innovation intermediaries can help company C find the resources it needs to bring one of its new technologies to market by allying with companies D and E. The intermediaries can be trusted to maintain confidentiality because if they ever violated the terms of an arrangement no company would hire them again.

Notes

1. Richard Leifer, Christopher M. McDermott, Gina Colarelli O'Connor, Lois S. Peters, Mark Rice, Robert W. Veryzer, *Radical Innovation: How Mature Companies Can Outsmart Upstarts* (Harvard Business School Press, 2000).

Originally published in August 2002
Reprint R0208E

The Sputtering R&D Machine

MARTHA CRAUMER

Executive Summary

HOMESTAR'S REPUTATION FOR BEING "the first, the best, the only" name in appliances is under threat. For the second time in six months, upstart competitor Vanguard has pulled off a market coup: Its retro line of refrigerators, ranges, and dishwashers is a huge hit. Meanwhile, HomeStar's latest big idea—jumbo appliances—is bombing. CEO Hal Marden is chagrined: How did the company lose its edge?

Kelly Dowd, HomeStar's head of marketing, blames Charlie Hamad, the company's chief engineer. Charlie is so focused on developing smart appliances—products that can cook, clean, and even shop—that he's lost touch with the changing marketplace, Kelly complains. Global competition is growing, and consumers' tastes are changing. Now, more than ever, churning out new products is critical to HomeStar's success.

But Charlie, a 27-year veteran who has spearheaded almost every major technological advance in the industry, pooh-poohs the new, flashy products: "Form over function. Nothing new there but a fancy paint job and higher prices."

Hal is torn. Charlie is a hero to him, but what if the market doesn't go for networked appliances? The company simply can't afford to put all its eggs in one basket. What's more, the biggest trade show of the year is just six months away, and HomeStar has nothing new to offer. Vanguard, meanwhile, is making product announcements every quarter. Is it time for Charlie to move on? How can HomeStar get its R&D efforts back on track?

Four commentators—Ideo's Tom Kelley, Whirlpool's Philip Pejovich, Thayer School of Engineering's Lewis Duncan, and Ealing Studios' John Kao—offer advice in this fictional case study.

As HAL MARDEN WATCHED his morning muffin spin slowly in the lunchroom microwave, he marveled at how this small appliance had forever changed the way people cook and eat. "The perfect invention," he mused to himself. "Small, fast, convenient, and energy-efficient. We thought microwaves would do away with conventional ovens. But instead, they became a whole new category of kitchen appliance."

After 25 years with HomeStar, Hal was still fascinated by the appliance business—and by the innovations that fueled it. As CEO for the last 12 years, he'd steadfastly maintained the company's commitment to research and development, vowing to uphold HomeStar's reputation for being "the first, the best, the only" name in appliances.

That's why the latest turn of events was so distressing.

Hal grabbed his coffee and muffin, retreated to his office, and closed the door, relieved that his assistant wasn't in yet. Then he reread the newspaper article. "Gaga for Retro," the headline proclaimed. "Vanguard, already the fastest-growing appliance maker in the country, has another major hit with its new retro line of refrigerators, ranges, and dishwashers. Rounded lines, chrome detailing, and colors like turquoise, yellow, and red give the appliances the look and feel of classic automobiles. And consumers seemingly can't get enough of them. 'We've got an emotional hit on our hands that cuts across demographic lines,' said a Vanguard spokesperson. 'People are having a love affair with these appliances. At the same time, we're showing old-schoolers like HomeStar that the industry can move beyond a needs-based market and appeal to consumers who follow trends and seek luxury.'"

Hal folded the paper and shook his head. As much as it pained him to see his company called "old school," he had to admit that HomeStar had stumbled lately. "We should've seen this coming," he thought. "For the last three years the auto industry has been looking back in time for inspiration. The PT Cruiser, the Mini Cooper, the VW Bug—all the biggest hits are riding a wave of nostalgia. How did we miss it? We're losing our edge."

This wasn't the first time HomeStar had been beaten to the punch. Just six months earlier, Vanguard had pulled off another coup: Its line of "Clean 'n' Eat" refrigerators had been the runaway hit of the Homebuilders trade show. Featuring a separate compartment for triple-washing and draining fruits and vegetables, the new line touted the importance of fresh produce and healthy eating and the dangers of lingering pesticides. The refrigerators flew off showroom floors.

Delicate Cycle

An urgent knock interrupted Hal's thoughts. "Come in,"
he answered wearily. Kelly Dowd, the company's head of
marketing, stomped into his office. "Did you read about
Vanguard?" she asked. "They've done it again—and
insulted us in the process. How are they getting these
products out so fast?"

"Well, they're not exactly technological breakthroughs," Hal smiled wryly. "But Vanguard does seem
to have a finger on the pulse of the consumer. They're
doing what we should be doing. It seems we've dropped
the ball."

"That's because we're focusing on the wrong things.
Charlie should pull his head out of the research lab and
knock on the kitchen doors of a few real people for a
change. He's obsessed with 'smart' appliances and this
'networked home' concept. But you know what? Except
for a handful of technogeeks, consumers aren't particularly interested. Most people we talk to couldn't care less."

Hal flinched. Charlie Hamad was one of his heroes. A
brilliant and visionary engineer, he'd headed HomeStar's
R&D unit for 27 years. Enormously respected outside the
company and beloved within it, he had spearheaded
almost every major technological advance in the industry; he was a key reason for HomeStar's past success.

"Look, Kelly," said Hal, "market research is your area.
So if there's a disconnect between what your group
thinks the market wants and what R&D is actually producing, then we need to work on fixing that. Remember,
Charlie's had a huge hand in making this company what
it is."

Kelly shook her head. "You mean making this company what it *was*. The market's changing, Hal. The rate

of product innovation is skyrocketing. Global competition is growing—those guys would love to eat us for lunch. And consumer tastes are changing. People want more choices. Some folks get a new car every two years. Why shouldn't they upgrade their appliances, too? We've got to get more new stuff out there, and fast."

Kelly was right. The market was changing dramatically. For years, innovation in the industry had focused on incremental gains—making appliances that were a little faster, a little quieter, or a little more efficient. As the products themselves became virtually interchangeable, the dominant players began competing on price, eroding profit margins. But in the last 18 months, a wave of innovation had washed over the industry. Appliance makers had begun recombining existing technologies to create entirely new products and designing them in appealing ways. Suddenly, the appliance industry was more like the consumer electronics industry; its rallying cry had become "to get customers to buy new products, create new products."

Now, more than ever, churning out new products was critical to HomeStar's success. But unfortunately, Charlie hadn't changed with the times. He pooh-poohed the new, flashy products—despite their higher profit margins, the fact that they encouraged consumers to upgrade more often, and their popularity with builders seeking the latest thing for their model homes. And that put HomeStar in the unenviable position of having to play catch-up.

"The next Homebuilders show is six months away," said Kelly. "If we don't roll out something new—something that gets people excited—we might as well kiss our reputation for innovation good-bye. We can't afford to lose our edge. Unless we want to go the way of the icebox."

Just then J.J. Knight, HomeStar's PR manager, poked her head into Hal's office. "Hey Hal, the 'What's New' section of *HomeView* magazine is on the line. Do we have anything for them this month?"

"Ouch! Sore subject, J.J. Tell them we do, but we can't talk about it right now—for competitive reasons."

Combustion Hazard

Charlie Hamad's office was a mess. A whiteboard covered with scribbles, flowcharts, and yellow Post-its spread across one wall. Stacks of magazines and files filled every inch of space. "Never trust a man with a tidy desk," he was fond of saying. "A tidy desk is the sign of an untidy mind." With a PhD in mechanical engineering and a passion for technology, Charlie oversaw Home-Star's global research, design, and product development groups. A wall filled with design and engineering awards attested to his record of accomplishment. Eccentric but brilliant, Charlie was a magnet for smart, dedicated scientists, designers, technologists, and engineers, and he inspired intense loyalty among his people.

Hal removed a pile of magazines from a chair and sat down. "Did you read about Vanguard's new retro line?" he asked.

Charlie snorted derisively. "Form over function. Nothing new there but a fancy paint job and higher prices."

"Consumers are jumping for joy."

"Wait till they see our networked appliances. Listen carefully, Hal." Charlie paused for effect. "The networked home is the future. These products will transform the way we live. They'll cook, clean, and shop for you—even do your household chores—using Internet technology. Imagine being able to automatically restock the fridge when you're out of food or download recipes right to your oven!"

"That's the future, Charlie. We need something now." Hal rubbed his eyes and sighed. "Look, we've got a problem. We're losing our position as industry leader. We haven't come up with anything new in months."

Charlie reminded Hal of the company's recent line of energy-saving washers, dryers, and dishwashers, inspired by the European market. Five years ago, Charlie had set up an R&D unit overseas to monitor market trends. It was—and continued to be—an expensive venture, but Charlie felt it was money well spent. He surmised that the fragmented and highly competitive nature of the overseas markets would drive innovations that hadn't yet hit the U.S. market—innovations that would shape the appliance industry's future. One of the first things he'd noticed was the growing popularity of energy-saving appliances in Europe, so he'd set about developing HomeStar's own line, despite opposition within the company.

"They're superb products, Charlie. From a technology standpoint, they're the best ones out there. And the margins are great—we can charge three times more for them. But ours were still in development when the first ones hit the U.S. market. Besides losing the early sales, we hurt our reputation for being 'the first.' What can we do to speed things up?"

"If you'll recall," Charlie said, "the folks in marketing were convinced that American consumers weren't interested in water- and energy-saving appliances, that they'd never pay the premium. Kelly kept pointing to the popularity of gas-guzzling SUVs as 'proof' that Americans weren't serious about conservation. I got the distinct message from you and from others that our energy-saving line wasn't a priority. Remember what got the big push instead? Jumbo appliances."

Hal winced and nodded. Someone in marketing had noticed the boom in "McMansions," those huge houses that people were building, often after tearing down more modest homes. That and the fact that every new house and major renovation project seemed to have at its heart a "great room"—a big, open space that combined the kitchen and living areas—had convinced a persistent and vocal group within the company that bigger is better in consumers' minds. But the jumbo appliances had bombed—the first major failure in HomeStar's history.

Charlie smiled smugly. "I don't need to remind you what a disaster that was. Meanwhile, our energy-saving appliances were a hit, and now you're asking me why it took so long. You need to trust my instincts, Hal."

"Your instincts are legendary, Charlie. That's not the issue. We've got the biggest trade show of the year in six months and nothing new to offer. Meanwhile, Vanguard is making new product announcements every quarter. The industry as a whole is moving toward fast-cycle innovation. If we can't keep up, we're sunk."

"Product extensions and paint jobs aren't innovations. The fact is, an elegant, technology-driven solution has its own time frame; it can't be rushed. And I've got my own reputation to consider. I don't develop crap. Never have, never will."

"Nobody wants you to develop 'crap.' But we need to make sure that we're developing products that consumers want. Frankly, I'm worried that you're devoting too many resources to networked appliances. What if the market doesn't bite? I don't want to put all our eggs in one basket. I'd like to see you and your people work more closely with marketing. I think you could learn a lot from each other—

recent missteps notwithstanding. Maybe you need more face time with them, Charlie." Hal looked at his watch. "Look, I've got a luncheon to get to. Let's talk some more when you get back from Europe next week."

Limited Warranty

Hal sank wearily into the back seat of a taxi, grateful for some time to think. It was increasingly clear that whatever had made HomeStar an industry leader in the past was no longer working. The market had changed, seemingly overnight. It felt as if everyone in the industry was playing by new rules—ones that HomeStar didn't have. Even worse, Charlie didn't seem to want them. Maybe it was time for new blood. But Charlie was a legend, an institution. Making any major change would feel like a betrayal.

Hal didn't usually have time for the Executive Roundtable luncheons, but he didn't want to miss this one. The featured speaker was Caroline Broderick, an old business school chum, and the subject was timely: "Is loyalty a liability? Managing in times of change."

Traffic was unusually light, and the taxi pulled in front of the City Club well before the opening reception. With time on his hands—a rare occurrence—Hal decided to indulge in some impromptu market research. Approaching

"Just keeping up on the latest technologies isn't enough anymore. You need more sizzle, less steak."

the maître d', he introduced himself and asked for a tour of the kitchen. Hal loved nothing more than talking to consumers of all stripes and observing how they cooked, cleaned, and interacted with their appliances. As he toured the kitchen, noting the oversized range that two sous-chefs were cooking on, Hal had a brainstorm. Pulling out a small notebook, he jotted down a note to himself: "Repackage and reposition jumbo appliances for institutional use?" Then he joined the reception in the dining room.

Hal sought out Caroline after her talk. "Good to see you!" he said warmly. "I enjoyed your presentation. But unfortunately, it hit a little too close to home." He briefly explained HomeStar's recent challenges.

Caroline nodded sympathetically. "It's tough when markets change and your people don't. Sounds like Charlie needs to develop some business savvy. Just keeping up on the latest technologies isn't enough anymore. You need more sizzle, less steak."

"It's hard to find someone who can do it all," said Hal. "But enough about business. How are your children?"

Caroline laughed. "My 'children' are 19 and 21 now. And I'm about to rejoin the workforce full time. Consulting and writing were great when the kids were younger and I wanted more flexibility, but I'm ready for something new." She hesitated, then continued. "I don't know how serious you are about making changes at HomeStar, Hal, but do you remember Peter Fortuna from B-school?"

"Of course! The man we thought would be a permanent student!" Hal said with a laugh. After getting a degree in computer science, an MBA, and a PhD in engineering, Peter had helped launch a very successful company that offered contract R&D services to a wide range of industries.

"Peter's company was just bought," said Caroline, "and I know he's looking for a new opportunity. Just something to think about."

The traffic on the way back to the office was slow and congested, like the tangle of thoughts in Hal's head. In his mind, there were two critical issues. The first was urgent and short term: How to come up with at least one hot new product for the trade show in six months when there was nothing in the pipeline. The second issue—and the most difficult challenge of his career—was how to fix R&D. "Is this just a funding and organizational problem that could be solved by a brainstorming session?" Hal wondered. "Or is it time for Charlie to move on?" Peter Fortuna's change of status offered a promising alternative. Maybe Charlie could be appointed chief technology officer and move away from running the whole show. "On the other hand, maybe I should drastically cut back the R&D group and outsource a larger piece of the pie," he mused. "Or maybe I'm simply being too impatient. Perhaps, as Charlie says, true innovation can't be rushed. If he's right about networked appliances and we get there first, we'll own a huge market."

It was time for some tough decisions.

How Can HomeStar Revitalize Its R&D Efforts?

Four commentators offer expert advice.

> TOM KELLEY *is the general manager of Ideo, a design and innovation firm based in Palo Alto, California. He is the author of* The Art of Innovation *(Doubleday, 2001).*

In a period of market transition, HomeStar has become the Cadillac of home appliances: prestigious and well built but lagging behind the times. Although the most urgent question facing CEO Hal Marden is about products, the underlying challenges are clearly about processes and people.

HomeStar's current business model is more technology-centered than customer-centered. The company's solid engineering worked well in an era when it had a distinct quality advantage and was selling the improved utility of its products. But while HomeStar's R&D department has been busy honing the next whiz-bang technology of networked appliances, there's been a sea change in consumer expectations. Quality is now assumed, which undermines the company's ability to maintain leadership on that basis. As consumers move up Maslow's hierarchy of needs, they are looking beyond mere utility; they want products that match their lifestyles and allow for self-expression.

"While HomeStar's R&D department has been busy honing the next whiz-bang technology of networked appliances, there's been a sea change in consumer expectations."

Just as Schwinn misjudged the shift to mountain bikes and Swiss watchmakers overlooked the value of quartz movements, HomeStar in general and Charlie Hamad in particular have been slow to realize that competitors and customers are redefining industry rules. As Kelly Dowd suggested, Charlie and his team need to get away from their desks and watch real people in real-life settings using the products of HomeStar and its competitors. Doing that will probably reveal all kinds of surprises, including some latent user needs.

For example, are all those retro fridges actually going into kitchens? Or does Vanguard have the best-selling *second* refrigerator in the industry, providing extra capacity for cold drinks in the basement or garage? If that's the case, HomeStar could beat Vanguard by offering products that are not only styled for those locations but also optimized for use as overflow space. Or Home-Star might create the twenty-first-century version of microwave ovens: small satellite products that don't replace existing appliances, just supplement them in convenient ways. The company's approach to innovation needs to be refreshed with a deeper understanding of customer needs and new insights into usage patterns.

As for the people problem, Kelly and Charlie display the classic split between marketing and R&D viewpoints. HomeStar won't be able to move forward on the innovation front until it narrows that divide. Given Charlie's stature in the company and his hero status with the CEO, phasing him out isn't a viable alternative, but Hal must find a way to change Charlie's attitude. His position that "I've got my own reputation to consider" suggests that Charlie himself is a barrier to innovation.

Since Charlie and Kelly are at an impasse, they need a stimulus to get them moving in the same direction. If they conducted field research with a cultural anthropologist, they'd gain insights into their customers—and learn from each other in the process. Working with a third party would also give Charlie and Kelly a chance to be on the same side of the table.

I'd also recommend that Hal retain Peter Fortuna or someone like him as a consultant to create rough prototypes for the upcoming trade show. HomeStar needs an infusion of fresh thinking, and a project like that might be just the thing to get the creative juices flowing again. Charlie's R&D team could still evaluate the prototypes and estimate production costs, but all feasible prototypes should be brought to the trade show and kept in a back room for key customers to evaluate. That way, HomeStar would get tangible customer feedback before fully committing resources to a product's development, and customers would feel that HomeStar values their feedback. It stands to reason that at least one prototype should be a networked appliance. HomeStar appears to be betting the company on networked products, but what it really needs is a portfolio of short- and long-term innovations.

With a continual flow of customer insights driving product innovation, HomeStar will be less likely to create today's equivalent of the pen-based computer craze: a fascinating technology in search of a customer need.

PHILIP PEJOVICH *is the vice president of growth and innovation for Whirlpool in Benton Harbor, Michigan. He was formerly Whirlpool's vice president for corporate technology and engineering development.*

HomeStar's issues go far beyond R&D's relationship with marketing, and they're deeper than deciding if Charlie is the right man for the job. HomeStar must rethink its whole approach to innovation. At Whirlpool, five basic tenets guide our efforts in this area—tenets that might serve HomeStar well.

The first tenet is to focus on the consumer. HomeStar is in the consumer products business, but it has taken its eye off the customer, allowing Vanguard to seize the advantage. HomeStar needs to spend more time assessing consumer needs, engaging consumers to experiment with possible solutions, and testing marketing concepts to assess their appeal. Most innovations fail for one of three reasons: They are not relevant to the consumer, they are difficult to distribute, or their value message is unclear. This first tenet is the most important, because innovation begins with the consumer.

The second tenet is to invite innovation from everywhere. Whirlpool's CEO views every employee as a consumer, so he has made innovation the responsibility of everyone in the organization. Every functional area—from finance to HR—has a performance goal tied to innovation. That has led not just to product innovations and brand extensions but also to innovations in how we communicate with consumers, how we sell to them, and how we provide service after the sale. HomeStar's CEO, by contrast, has a very traditional view of product development. Hal believes that innovation is owned by R&D. That mind-set keeps him from tapping into a rich source of ideas—his own people at all levels of the organization.

"Hal believes that innovation is owned by R&D. That mind-set keeps him from tapping into a rich sources of ideas— his own people at all levels of the organization."

The third tenet is to take a portfolio view of product innovation. The innovation pipeline is critical to a company's future. Hal's dilemma—coming up with one hot new product when the pipeline is empty—is the entire management team's fault, not just Charlie's. HomeStar should waste no time in creating a portfolio of opportunities—some short term, some long term, some incremental, some disruptive. Once the portfolio is created, HomeStar's management team must ask: "Can we maintain our 'first, best, only' position given our current plans?" Balance is critical. Portfolios with an excessive focus on technology risk losing touch with the marketplace and falling into the "build it and they will come" mind-set. But portfolios heavily weighted with incremental product improvements that simply respond to market pull are no better. This me-too approach jeopardizes HomeStar's leadership position. The company, therefore, needs to carefully manage its portfolio of product innovations.

Speed is the fourth tenet. Traditionally, product development has three basic steps: scope and size, approve and fund, and execute. But companies that take that approach risk fully funding a project before they know if it's truly viable. That's why, at Whirlpool, we conduct a series of customer experiments before committing our full resources to a project. These experiments help us learn quickly and cheaply what works and what doesn't, and they help push decision making much further downstream. Initial concepts get refined before major investments are made, and we get to market more quickly with products that better meet consumer needs. HomeStar could achieve much faster time to market by adopting a similar approach, but it would require a major cultural shift.

The fifth tenet is to manage intellectual property. Given HomeStar's commitment to R&D, it has an opportunity to create a sustainable competitive advantage by developing an intellectual property strategy. In the networked home appliances area, for example, HomeStar is probably in a position to develop a broad array of patents that could be used either as a barrier to entry or—even better—as a way to attract competitors into an emerging market while extracting additional value. As the appliance industry becomes more innovative and the pace of change accelerates, the creation, protection, and licensing of intellectual property will become even more critical to HomeStar's success.

By following these tenets, HomeStar can reestablish its leadership position, generate significant customer loyalty, and create value for its shareholders.

LEWIS DUNCAN *is the dean of the Thayer School of Engineering at Dartmouth College in Hanover, New Hampshire.*

HomeStar's success is based on product innovation; its future hinges on its ability to convert ideas into invoices. Its challenges today are more ones of execution than invention. The friendly advice that HomeStar needs "more sizzle, less steak" is only half right; it needs more of both.

Consider the company from a technology perspective. HomeStar has an accomplished R&D group led by a brilliant, experienced, and visionary director. The group attracts smart and dedicated scientists, designers, and engineers. Its corporate culture promotes creativity and loyalty. Its history of innovation secures HomeStar's leadership standing in the marketplace. And now the group is well positioned at the forefront of smart appliances, an emerging technology that promises to transform the whole industry. HomeStar's long-term advantage over global competitors clearly depends upon its continued R&D strength.

"The friendly advice that HomeStar needs 'more sizzle, less steak' is only half right; it needs more of both."

But while its future may rely upon innovation, its present market share does not. HomeStar has several immediate problems to deal with. Organizationally, the company must separate the process of continuous product improvement from the distinct R&D process of intermittent product innovation. Operationally dysfunctional, the sluggish product design effort at HomeStar threatens the company's survival as it competes against more agile competitors such as Vanguard. In the current business environment, HomeStar must become a much faster company.

To that end, HomeStar should move product design into its own division and make it responsible for working with marketing, sales, and manufacturing to anticipate, identify, and respond to emergent market trends. In addition, an independent design team must be empowered to move quickly so that it can deliver the "sizzle." That's what will keep HomeStar appearing in the monthly issues of *HomeView* magazine and help it remain a fresh presence at the Homebuilders shows.

Longer term, HomeStar's R&D team will be expected to provide the "steak." To prosper as a technology-based company, HomeStar must lead. Mercurial customer trends won't provide the farsighted guidance for transformational change; the vision of the engineers already at work in HomeStar's research laboratories will. Their passion for innovation will lead to the inventions that become the mother of future consumer necessity.

Finally, HomeStar must address some awkward personnel issues. Hal has not exhibited leadership yet, and he must—soon. Also a problem is Kelly, the head of marketing. Her misrepresentation of the research enterprise is administratively corrosive. It was her department that steered HomeStar into the disastrous jumbo appliances. It was also apparently marketing's misdirection that slowed HomeStar's development of the energy-efficient appliances, a "first and best" prospect missed despite the R&D team's early identification of the opportunity. And were the modest "retro" and "healthy eating" product configuration changes really supposed to come out of the corporate research labs?

Kelly is right about one thing: The industry demands much faster product cycle times. But she's wrong to blame Charlie for the company's recent missteps. In fact, Charlie seems to be the only person at HomeStar who's trying to anticipate trends, although the European R&D lab may be an inappropriate luxury for that purpose.

Yes, Charlie needs to appreciate the speed of modern business cycles, but he is essential to the company's long-term vitality. Reassigning him and bringing in Peter Fortuna to oversee R&D is unnecessary and could even be destructive. Peter might, however, be an excellent candidate to run a product design division because he holds the right balance of business and engineering credentials to serve as a bridge between the disparate marketing and technology cultures.

Through continued innovation, HomeStar has every opportunity to remain the leader in the appliance industry. And in the long run, the company is likely to discover that loyalty only becomes a liability when it is misplaced or lost.

JOHN KAO *is the chairman of Ealing Studios in London and the managing director of Kao & Company in San Francisco. He is the author of* Jamming: The Art and Discipline of Business Creativity *(HarperBusiness, 1996).*

Poor Hal. The competitive tempo of the industry has picked up, and now HomeStar is on the defensive. Nimble competitors are making appliances that reflect greater insight into customer preferences, and what's more, they're getting those products to market quickly. One is reminded of Apple's use of form, color, and graphic design as competitive weapons in a gray PC world.

Hal has a range of problems that, sadly, affect myriad companies in all industries. First is the lack of a strategy. HomeStar faces a make-or-break trade show in just six months, and its pipeline is empty. It's shocking that the CEO has nothing to say to a leading industry publication. This is a sign of how far the company has fallen. Hal's second problem is HomeStar's lack of connection to its customers. The company was late to the green and clean trend, plunged into jumbo appliances (which bombed), missed the retro trend, and is now preparing a networked appliance plan that already has the odor of failure about it.

As an organization, HomeStar is dysfunctional. Hal has failed to harness the creative energy latent in the inevitable disagreements between marketing and R&D. He needs to find a way to integrate diverse viewpoints, either through a strategic-planning process or perhaps by fundamentally rethinking the company's approach to R&D. Sequential, linear processes must give way to networks of collaboration and communities of interest that form around projects.

Charlie is both an asset and a liability, with an emphasis on the latter. He's opinionated, he cares more about his reputation than the company's, and he's at the center of a cult of personality that is both his power base and a creative bottleneck. His infatuation with technology and his seat-of-the-pants approach are risk factors for the company.

"Hal must make quick, assured, tough decisions— not a great fit with his Hamlet-like indecisiveness."

Charlie does, however, have the right idea about the importance of a global perspective. But having an international R&D unit isn't the best approach. Instead, HomeStar might develop some form of global customer insight and environmental-sensing capabilities—whether in-house or outsourced—and set up centralized R&D and manufacturing capabilities in the most cost-effective parts of the world.

HomeStar also needs to think about how to manage a portfolio of customers and innovation initiatives. Certainly some consumers will respond to price. Others will respond to features, and still others to design elements. Service isn't mentioned in this case study, but it would seem to be key to cultivating customer loyalty. And what about creating an upgrade path for its customers? HomeStar needs to decide whether it's in the business of products or relationships.

As I see it, Hal has three major challenges. First, he must find a way to rally the troops, reinvigorate the strategy process, and chart a course of action. The good news is that there is turbulence in the marketplace and therefore an opportunity to reassert HomeStar's "first, best" ethos. The bad news is that "same old" just won't cut it. Hal must make quick, assured, tough decisions—not a great fit with his Hamlet-like indecisiveness.

Second, Hal needs to radically reframe the company's innovation processes. He must see himself as the manager of an innovation portfolio with a range of time frames, business models, and customers. He needs to get something into the pipeline that steals a march on his competitors. And he has to consider the company's long-term goals when contemplating a set of disruptive innovations.

Finally, he needs to take decisive action on the talent side. Only a blind person could fail to see the moss that has grown on Charlie during his 27-year tenure. Hal needs new people, including outsiders, as well as radically reframed processes to capture customer insights. Perhaps he should bump Charlie upstairs to Senior Fellow status, bring in Peter Fortuna as a contractor, and look to fresh talent for new product ideas. HomeStar needs more divergence on the idea front and more convergence on the implementation side.

Originally published in August 2002
Reprint R0208A

Inspiring Innovation

ELLEN PEEBLES

Executive Summary

SOME ORGANIZATIONS REPEATEDLY come up with great ideas, even though each act of innovation is really a leap of imagination that can't be taught or predicted. But even if they can't exactly replicate those successes, can other organizations learn from them? HBR's editors asked 16 innovation experts, leaders but not necessarily inventors themselves, one question: "What's the one thing you've done that most inspired innovation in your organization?"

Some of them—like Nolan Bushnell, who founded Atari; CEO Michael Dell; and venture capitalist Esther Dyson—emphasize the importance of letting people experiment and take risks. Giving employees plenty of room to make mistakes creates opportunities for serendipity and valuable learning. That sentiment is echoed by Mark Dean, an IBM Fellow and inventor,

89

who says his company encourages its researchers not to draw boundaries but to keep reaching for and pursuing the most promising ideas.

Hal Tovin, an executive vice president of a financial group, and John Talley, a pharmaceutical researcher, believe that hiring people with widely divergent skills and talents sets the stage for increased innovation. Proctor & Gamble's Craig Wynett proposes approaching innovation systematically, just as executives would any business issue: Define a problem and then solve it. Larry Keeley, the president of an innovation strategy firm, encourages others to innovate not only in the realm of products but also in customer service, business models, and networking. Luciano Maiani, the director general of the European Organization for Nuclear Research (CERN), states the case for pure science by claiming that it drives innovation as much as markets do.

These experts and others pull back the curtain on the mysteries of innovation to show that concrete, deliberate actions can enhance the possibility for increased creativity and productivity in your company.

It's one of the toughest challenges an executive faces: How do you get your people to think creatively—to challenge the status quo—while still keeping your everyday operations running smoothly? Innovation is not like most other business functions and activities. There are no reliable templates, rules, processes, or even measures of success. In a sense, each act of innovation is a unique feat, a leap of the individual—or the collective—imagination that can be neither predicted nor replicated. Innovation, in short, is anything but business as usual.

And yet certain organizations are somehow able to come up with great ideas over and over again. Some of the ideas are for new products, some for new ways of working, others are for new strategies, still others for entirely new lines of business. Is there a secret to these companies' successes? Can other organizations learn from their examples? To find out, we turned to the people most qualified to answer—not necessarily inventors (although you'll find a few of them in the group) but those who've been able to inspire others to creative genius. We asked them a single question: "What's the one thing you've done that most inspired innovation in your organization?" Here's what they had to say.

Make It the Norm

CRAIG WYNETT *is the general manager of future growth initiatives at Procter & Gamble in Cincinnati.*

W HAT WE'VE DONE TO ENCOURAGE innovation is make it ordinary. By that I mean we don't separate it from the rest of our business. Many companies make innovation front-page news, and all that special attention has a paradoxical effect. By serving it up as something exotic, you isolate it from what's normal. Companies don't trumpet their quality assurance processes or their packaging as special practices because they're part of the fiber of what they do—they're ordinary business. The same has to be true of innovation. Too many times we've seen corporate innovation programs that are the business equivalent of football's Hail Mary pass—they start with all kinds of hope and excitement, but in the end they rarely produce results. And why would they? For innovation to be reliable, it needs to be addressed systematically, like any business issue in which you define the problem and then solve it: What do we want to accomplish, and how? What resources will we need? Who will be on the team? How do we motivate and reward them? And how will we measure success?

Today's most sought-after business talent is the ability to originate. But the perception of the creative process is still based on self-limiting assumptions about eureka lightbulbs flashing over the head of some inspired genius rather than the well-managed diligence of ordinary people. At P&G, we think of creativity not as a mysterious gift of the talented few but as the everyday task of making nonobvious connections—bringing together things that don't normally go together. One way to do that is to look at contradictions in the marketplace. For example, we developed a product called ThermaCare, a disposable heating pad that provides regulated low-level heat for at least eight hours. How'd we come up with it? Lots of aging baby boomers out there have all kinds of creaks and muscle twinges. Drugs can treat the pain, but they can also create other problems, like stomach ailments. So you have a contradiction: People don't want to live with pain, but they don't want to take painkillers. We saw that contradiction in the market and viewed it as an invitation to create a breakthrough product, one that resolves a paradox without requiring any trade-offs. You can see how opportunities like this can come up in just about any industry. In the telecommunications business, before call waiting, for example, you could either talk on the phone or receive phone calls but not both.

A final word of caution. Isolating innovation from mainstream business can produce a dangerous cultural side effect: Creativity and leadership can be perceived as opposites. This artificial disconnect means that innovators often lack the visibility and clout to compete for the resources necessary for success. Only when innovators operate with the credibility of leaders will innovation become a productive part of everyday business.

Put Aside Ego

THOMAS FOGARTY *invented the first balloon catheter to be used therapeutically. He practices cardiovascular surgery at Stanford University Medical Center; creates companies that develop and market his medical device designs; and is a cofounder of Three Arch Partners, a VC firm in Portola Valley, California, that funds medical start-ups.*

The most important thing, I've found, is to help people broaden their perspective. In medicine, the definition of a better way to do something often depends on whether you're the giver or the recipient of care. For example, I'm involved in a company that diagnoses sleep apnea. Currently, a patient has to subject himself to what's known as a diagnostic sleep lab. He's taken out of his normal environment—his home—and put into an artificial environment where he's hooked up to three separate monitors that check heart rate, breathing, and blood oxygen levels and attached to myriad other devices. It costs him $2,000. A physician would say, "That's how to make the diagnosis; what's wrong with

"One of the hardest things about innovation is getting people to accept that the way they work just might not be the best."

it?" But if you talked to a patient, you'd find there's a whole lot wrong with it. Consequently, if you want to improve the experience from the patient's perspective, you'd make the diagnostic procedure less expensive and intrusive, and you'd make it available in his home.

Getting people to expand their views—to see a situation through others' eyes—often raises ego issues. People don't want to believe that they're doing things in ways that are less than optimal. In fact, one of the hardest things about innovation is getting people to accept that the way they work just might not be the best.

Mix People Up

LIEUTENANT GENERAL RONALD T. KADISH *is the director of the Missile Defense Agency in the U.S. Department of Defense. The MDA is responsible for acquiring ballistic missile defense systems for the U.S. armed forces.*

One of the surest ways to get a job done more innovatively is, quite simply, to reorganize frequently. When you put people into a new structure, it stimulates them to rethink what they're doing on a day-to-day basis.

I've reorganized the Missile Defense Agency on a major scale twice in less than two years. Why? We needed to transform ourselves from an organization dedicated to scientific experimentation to one focused on the design and acquisition of weapons. The technologies we'd been working on for 20 years had become sufficiently mature that we could actually start developing effective systems, and the geopolitical environment had changed to the point where we had a mandate to move forward. We needed to orient people toward a new goal, and reorganizing was one way to do that.

It's traumatic for most people, especially in very hierarchical organizations like ours. But on balance, I find that people respond well if you can get them to focus not on the inconveniences of restructuring but on the satisfaction of setting high goals and then knocking down the barriers to achieving them.

Don't Fear Failure

MICHAEL DELL *is the founder, chairman, and CEO of Dell Computer in Austin, Texas.*

At Dell, innovation is about taking risks and learning from failure. Today, we're well known for inventory management, logistics, supply chain management, and such, but that wasn't always the case. Back in 1989, we had a very large disaster—large, at least, for the small company we were at the time. The personal computer industry was making the transition to a new type of memory chip, and we found ourselves stuck with far too many of the old kind. That was a

"You need to encourage innovation when your company's doing well. The last thing you want to do when you're in the lead is become complacent."

costly mistake, and it took us about a year to recover, but we learned from it. The failure led us to develop a new way to manage inventory, and we went from being last place in the minor leagues to where we now win the World Series every year.

To tap into that kind of innovation, we do our best to make sure that people aren't afraid of the possibility of failure, and we do a lot of experiments. For instance, one of our managers in the consumer group came up with the idea to offer installation service to consumers in order to reach people who might be apprehensive about setting up a new computer. The idea seemed like it would help out a group of customers, and it made a lot of sense from a cost standpoint as well. We knew from our experience with business customers that when our staff installs a computer, the incidence of set-up failures is almost zero. The consumer team threw around the idea, did a pilot with one group of salespeople, and found out what worked and what didn't. Within two weeks, we'd made this service available to every consumer in the United States. I actually found out about this by accident—it wasn't something that we had a bunch of meetings about in boardrooms. Incremental improvements and experiments happen all the time.

One other thing: You need to encourage innovation when your company's doing well. The last thing you want to do when you're in the lead is become complacent.

Hire Outsiders

HAL TOVIN *is the group executive vice president of the Emerging Channels Division of Citizens Financial Group, headquartered in Providence, Rhode Island. He directs the bank's ATM and debit card business, in-store banking, business banking, and on-line banking and Internet strategy.*

The most important step I've taken to encourage innovation is to hire people who have experience outside of banking—creative people who can apply what they've learned in dynamic, customer-centric categories to our more traditional businesses. For example, our in-store banking business—we've put full-service branches into grocery stores—is run by a person with a sales and marketing background. Our ATM business is run by someone who used to be in real estate. I myself am a classically trained marketer of packaged goods.

Employing people with diverse skills and talents helps us challenge the status quo when developing business strategies. Most banks, for example, look at in-store banking as a service for existing customers. We take a very different view; we use our grocery store branches to acquire new customers. We hire people from retail stores like the Gap, Macy's, and Starbucks and screen them for what we call BVAC characteristics: bright, verbal, assertive, creative. The staff go into the grocery aisles wearing their Citizens aprons, pushing their Citizens grocery carts with promotional offers, and getting into friendly conversations. Their objective is to develop relationships with store customers. Then when shoppers have banking needs, they'll find a familiar face at the bank. The result is that we've built a billion-dollar bank in just our in-store branches.

Abandon the Crowd

LARRY KEELEY *is the president of Doblin, an innovation strategy firm with offices in Chicago and San Francisco.*

A nearly universal misconception about innovation is that the ideal goal is to create the next hot product. That's why most companies focus their R&D dollars there. But because it's increasingly easy for other companies to copy any new product, you rarely get a return on those investments. So the principal thing we've done to encourage innovation is to help people see that there are actually many types of innovation—product innovation is one type, but so is innovation in customer service, in business models, in networking, and so on.

Consider the Chrysler minivan. Chrysler developed it at a time when the company was on the verge of bankruptcy. It created the van as a platform and depended on a network of suppliers to develop family-oriented advances that could be plugged into the platform—video games, removable seats, integral baby seats that fold down so beleaguered parents don't have to wrestle with them. The suppliers had to bear the cost of the R&D. That's an example not of product innovation but of networking innovation.

"You can actually spend less and make more money in innovation if you pay attention to the valleys, those places your competitors have overlooked."

Companies miss out on all sorts of opportunities for innovation because they focus so closely on their competitors. If you map out the different types of innovation activity in a given industry, you'll almost always find that most organizations are concentrating on the same types—they're all investing in the same things, just to keep up. There may be a lot of activity in customer service innovation, for example, but nothing's happening in networking.

Mapping innovation activity gives you a sense of the terrain—the peaks and valleys in investments and actions. There's an old saying that "there's gold in them thar hills." Well, there may be even more gold in them thar valleys. You can actually spend less and make more money in innovation if you pay attention to the valleys, those places your competitors have overlooked.

Let Go of Your Ideas

NOLAN BUSHNELL *is the CEO of uWink, an entertainment and game network located in Los Angeles. A longtime Silicon Valley pioneer, he founded Atari, the world's first video game company, in the early 1970s. He is also the founder of Chuck E. Cheese's Pizza Time Theater.*

I think it's essential to build a culture where there's no such thing as a bad idea. At uWink, for example, we have regular "compost" sessions to come up with new game ideas. We don't debate their value. Our priority is simply to get as many ideas as possible out of individuals' heads and into the group's heads. The ideas then become collective problems or puzzles that percolate throughout the group. And a couple of months later, someone—very often not the person who came up with a particular idea—has a breakthrough insight that allows us to move forward. In software, especially, the best ideas lose their owners and take on lives of their own.

We have very fast product life cycles, so I believe in a tough love approach to new product development. Give people too much time, and a project can become a breeding ground for internal politics. Likewise, too much money can become a crutch for creative thinking. Firm deadlines and tight budgets keep people focused on creating viable products and getting them to market as soon as possible. There's no substitute for getting something on the shelves and hearing what customers have to say. The true test of any innovation is how the market-place responds.

Don't Underestimate Science

LUCIANO MAIANI *is the director general of the European Organization for Nuclear Research (CERN), based in Geneva. Some 6,500 scientists, half of the world's particle physicists from laboratories and universities all over the globe, do research at CERN.*

Our primary obstacle to innovation is getting funding. There's a general belief among non-scientists that particle physics will not yield the kind of commercial applications that physics research did in the twentieth century. Very often I hear from member states that provide funding to CERN, "What could we possibly do with an understanding of quarks?" My answer is that pure science always drives innovation just as much as markets do. An incredible amount of technology transfer happens during R&D, when we're building the advanced tools needed for large-scale experiments. The most well-known example is the protocol for the Web, which was developed at CERN. But there's also a range of potentially promising applications—medical-imaging applications, for example—coming out of the R&D from our accelerator, the Large Hadron Collider.

I always try to make technology transfer very visible by urging our research scientists to file patents on their R&D breakthroughs and to seek out joint ventures to develop commercial applications. As a particle physicist, I know the value of pure science. But in this day and age, it's wrong to argue that pure science is all that matters. Science and technology go hand in hand.

Fight Negativity

MIKE LAZARIDIS is the founder, president, and co-CEO of Research In Motion, a maker of a range of wireless solutions including BlackBerry, which connects users to their corporate e-mail and to other information through wireless data networks. The company is located in Waterloo, Ontario.

Innovation is like professional sports: It looks easy, but when you're on the field, you see how complicated and difficult it is. To me, the key is building conviction. Few companies have the conviction to proceed down a path in the face of differing opinions from the industry, competitors, analysts, and the media. When companies get discouraged by these challenges and lose conviction, they make mistakes.

Also, one of my cardinal rules is, "Always hire people who are smarter than you." I tell people, don't worry about your job. Find people who can do it better than you.

Ask "What If?"

MARK DEAN is an IBM Fellow and the vice president of systems of IBM Research in Yorktown Heights, New York. An engineer and inventor, he has more than 30 patents or patents pending, including three of IBM's nine original PC patents.

Since December 1999, IBM has been working on a project called Blue Gene, which is a computer designed to model the protein-folding process in genetics. That work will require a huge advance in computing power, and we're using a radical approach to allow a very small machine to perform more than one quadrillion operations per second (a petaflop). Moore's law—that the amount of information able to be stored on a transistor will double every 18 months—predicts that it will take us 15 years to produce those calculations, but we're on course to deliver them in five.

We can aim for this kind of breakthrough at IBM because the company places very few constraints on its researchers. We are continually encouraged to spend time exploring new ideas and asking "what if?" questions, and we're allowed to pursue the ones we think have the most promise. For instance, the PC/AT that IBM launched in 1984—which featured an enhanced way to make peripherals work efficiently with a PC or PC compatible—was developed from something I'd been doing in my spare time. I have to say the only constraint I've ever felt deeply is the number of hours in the day.

"Researchers always want to go for that last 2% of performance. But it's better to get a sufficient solution out fast and then continue to enhance it."

I try to create that same unconstrained environment in the project teams I oversee. I do, of course, try to provide focus, set reasonable goals, and map out timelines. I also stress the importance of getting something out there, even if the product isn't 100% of what we envisioned. Researchers always want to go for that last 2% of performance, but I have to remind them that it's better to get a sufficient solution out fast and then continue to enhance it. My main role, though, is not to draw the boundaries but to encourage people to keep reaching. People have a lot of great ideas, if you give them space to do their thing and create an environment that is collaborative, not competitive—if you never say "that's silly" when they're thinking out of the box.

Merge Patience and Passion

JOHN TALLEY *is the vice president of drug discovery at Microbia in Cambridge, Massachusetts. He led the chemistry team at Pharmacia that found Celebrex, an anti-arthritis drug, and received the Pharmaceutical Research and Manufacturers of America Discoverers Award 2002.*

I have been able to foster among people on my team a passion for our work. You need that passion because

"If the tools you're working with are hammers, you don't want all problems to be seen as nails."

what we do is just so darned hard. Almost 80% of the people who go into medicinal chemistry retire never having worked on a discovery that leads to a

commercial product. So if you get bummed out every time you make a lousy compound, you're going to have a pretty miserable life.

A mandatory partner to passion is diversity. People with different scientific backgrounds will bring different frames of reference to a problem and can spark an exciting and dynamic exchange of ideas. If the tools you're working with are hammers, you don't want all problems to be seen as nails.

The science is just so much more interesting with passion and diversity. Look at what happened when we worked on Celebrex. Ever since aspirin was introduced in the United States at the end of the nineteenth century, chemists have been trying to make better nonsteroidal anti-inflammatory compounds. One problem everyone's encountered is that the enzyme that causes painful inflammation also helps protect the stomach lining from digestive acids. So when a painkiller blocks inflammation, it also can cause serious gastrointestinal problems.

Some of our colleagues had evidence that the form of the enzyme that induced inflammation was slightly different from that which protected the stomach, so we set out to find a molecular compound that would block only the form that induced inflammation. We went down so many fruitless alleys and made a lot of dead-end compounds. We combed through mountains of literature to see if someone had once made such a compound and not known it. Sure enough, we found a compound created in the early 1980s that partially inhibited this enzyme. That was one of those eureka days. But we were now about 2% of the way there; we still had to find out how to turn the compound into a safe and effective drug. Even when we put the drug into clinical trials, we didn't expect to know for years whether it would make it to market.

In fact, Celebrex had an almost record journey from the lab bench to the pharmacy shelf: seven years from the time we started work on the project. In an environment with these kinds of time frames, you need passion to sustain you. Nevertheless, it's important that your passion not blind you to the fact that sometimes you need to kill a project—and kill it fast. Before our chemistry team began working on what turned out to be Celebrex, we were working on a blood pressure drug. Although it was clear that that research ultimately wouldn't yield a product, some people on the team had emotional attachments to the technology and had a hard time letting it go. But if we hadn't moved on, we wouldn't have Celebrex.

Outsmart Your Customers

MARCIAN E. "TED" HOFF *is the chief technologist of the consulting firm FTI/Teklicon in San Jose, California. One of the first employees of Intel, he is credited with being an inventor of the microprocessor.*

You have to be able to bend the rules. Back in the 1960s, when I was with Intel, a calculator company named Busicom asked us to manufacture a set of 12 custom chips for some new calculators it was planning to introduce. Each chip would be dedicated to performing a single function. I hadn't worked on calculators before, and I was surprised to see the complexity of their design. I wondered if it would be possible to have one chip, a general-purpose central processor, that could be programmed to do all the functions. My frame of reference was some recent minicomputer designs, which were very simple but which enabled you to do a lot of complex things. To its credit, Intel's upper management was open enough to let me experiment with my idea. Those managers allowed me to break a cardinal rule of business: Always do what the customer wants. We didn't do what the customer wanted. We did something better.

Experiment Like Crazy

BETTY COHEN *is a corporate strategist for the Youth Segment at the Turner Broadcasting System. She is also the founder and former president of Cartoon Network Worldwide. Both organizations are headquartered in Atlanta.*

My favorite way to encourage innovation is to take an experimental approach to R&D. A couple of years ago, the cable world was abuzz with talk of convergence, but nobody really knew what that meant. Since it was a brave new world, we recognized that we had to

experiment with a variety of experiences for Cartoon
Network fans that brought together on-air and on-line
participation with the channel. I encouraged my TV
and on-line creative leaders to plot three different
approaches to the future, and I also set an expectation of learning, knowing that some ideas would play better than others but that we'd end up with insight about why

"What prevents innovation? The dangerous brew of fear and complacency— staying where you are out of fear of failing, of blowing too much money, or of placing the wrong bets."

each played like it did. And then we tested everything—
from simulcasting Web and TV versions of the same
cartoon character premier to a live on-line viewer
request weekend to a more interactive on-line action
and adventure show.

What prevents innovation? The dangerous brew of
fear and complacency—staying where you are out of fear
of failing, of blowing too much money, or of placing the
wrong bets.

Make It Meaningful

DANIEL VASELLA *trained as a physician and is now the chairman and chief executive officer of Novartis, a pharmaceutical company based in Basel, Switzerland.*

One way we try to foster innovation—both the technological innovation that leads to new drugs and the
organizational innovation that improves the way we do
business—is to align our business objectives with our
ideals. Doing so reaches people's intrinsic motivation.
Certainly, extrinsic motivation is important; we offer

stock options to our scientists and sponsor company research awards that enhance a researcher's visibility both within and outside Novartis. But I believe that people also do a better job when they believe in what they do and in how the company behaves, when they see that their work does more than enrich shareholders.

In the past few years, we have complemented our goal of economic value creation with another goal: good worldwide corporate citizenship. So while we're developing what we hope will be blockbuster drugs for the developed world, we've agreed, for example, to donate our leprosy multidrug therapy to the World Health Organization until the disease is eradicated. We also recognize that many ailments pervading the poorest countries are neglected diseases, with few R&D resources dedicated to finding treatments. With this in mind, we founded a research center in Singapore that focuses on developing drugs to treat diseases such as dengue hemorrhagic fever and tuberculosis; in all likelihood, such drugs will be barely profitable at best.

"People do a better job when they believe in what they do and in how the company behaves, when they see that their work does more than enrich shareholders."

These activities have deep meaning for our employees and unleash their energy and enthusiasm. With regard to our breakthrough cancer drug Glivec (called Gleevec in the United States), for instance, our researchers overcame every obstacle to develop the drug, and our production teams worked around the clock to produce enough supply for clinical trials. The alignment of objectives, ideals, and values contributes greatly to the motivation and thereby the energy that employees at all levels, myself included, devote to their work.

Stop the Bickering

DAVID FALVEY *is the executive director of the British Geological Survey, which has its headquarters in Keyworth, Nottingham, United Kingdom. In 2001, the organization was named to Vision 100, a listing by British Telecommunications of the most innovative organizations in the United Kingdom.*

When I joined the British Geological Survey in 1998, I found a hierarchical organization structured around the various disciplines and subdisciplines in geology. These had developed into competing empires, and collaboration on creative approaches to a customer problem was, at worst, unthinkable, and, at best, forced.

The key to spurring a wave of innovation was creating a structure and climate that ended the internal competition. I stopped the rivalries between divisions not by dismantling the divisions but by eliminating people's affiliation with them—I created a matrix structure. A program, headed by a manager, would be responsible for a range of projects. But the people working on those projects would come from a human resource pool whose allegiance would be to the mission of the organization rather than to a specific program. Just as I think of myself as an Australian rather than as a citizen of Sydney or New South Wales, so our scientists ideally feel like members of the BGS community rather than, for example, the Economic Minerals and Geochemical Baselines Program.

The structural change, in addition to eliminating internal competition, heightened our external competitive focus, which fostered increased innovation. Because the new program managers no longer "own" staff members, they have to devise projects that are interesting enough to attract people. Furthermore, because staff members don't have enforced loyalties to particular groups, they feel free to speak up with suggestions that can benefit the entire organization.

That change wasn't easy. People hated letting go of their identification with specific divisions. And I was a foreigner coming into a very old organization—one founded in 1835. When you're a new chum, you can't just walk in and say, "Right, guys, we're going to do it this way now"—unless you bring a sledgehammer. So we spent two years in discussions, gradually winning consensus for the change. The change was more orchestrated than directed by me; the orchestra members brought about change for themselves.

Don't Innovate, Solve Problems

ESTHER DYSON *is the chairman of New York–based EDventure Holdings and the author of* Release 2.0: A Design for Living in the Digital Age. *She is an active investor in and adviser to a wide range of young IT companies in the United States and Europe.*

I question the assumption that companies should try to inspire innovation. I don't try to encourage creativity for creativity's sake; instead, I try to encourage creative solutions to real problems. Innovation is good only if it's useful. Some companies reorganize every six months just to do something different. What they really need is better internal communication, not a new reporting structure.

So how do you encourage useful innovation? By doing two things. One, you have to promote risk taking—be open to experimentation and philosophical about things that go wrong. My motto is, "Always make new mistakes." There's no shame in making a mistake. But then learn from it and don't make the same one again. Everything I've learned, I've learned by making mistakes.

And two, you have to give people a reason to be enthusiastic about trying new tools, whether you're selling the tools or trying to get them used internally. One mistake I made was to think that people would be eager to use e-mail and other collaboration tools. But it's actually very hard to change people's habits. One way to get people to use new things is to have the chairman use them—if the chairman is in the hallway talking about something in an e-mail he or she just received, other people in the company will focus on that result and start using it. Experimentation has to start at the top.

Originally published in August 2002
Reprint R0208B

The Discipline of Innovation

PETER F. DRUCKER

Executive Summary

HOW MUCH OF INNOVATION is inspiration, and how much is hard work? The answer lies somewhere in the middle, says management thinker Peter Drucker. In this HBR classic from 1985, he argues that innovation is real work that can and should be managed like any other corporate function. Success is more likely to result from the systematic pursuit of opportunities than from a flash of genius.

Indeed, most innovative business ideas arise through the methodical analysis of seven areas of opportunity. Within a company or industry, opportunities can be found in unexpected occurrences, incongruities of various kinds, process needs, or changes in an industry or market. Outside a company, opportunities arise from demographic changes, changes in perception, or new knowledge. There is some overlap among the sources, and the potential for innovation may well lie in more than one area at a time. Innovations based on new knowledge tend to have the greatest effect on the marketplace, but it often takes decades before the ideas are translated into actual products, processes, or services. The other sources of innovation are easier and simpler to handle, yet they still require managers to look beyond established practices, Drucker explains.

The author emphasizes that innovators need to look for simple, focused solutions to real problems. The greatest praise an innovation can receive is for people to say, "That's so obvious!" Grandiose ideas designed to revolutionize an industry rarely work. Innovation, like any other endeavor, takes talent, ingenuity, and knowledge. But Drucker cautions that if diligence, persistence, and commitment are lacking, companies are unlikely to succeed at the business innovation.

How much of innovation is inspiration, and how much is hard work? If it's mainly the former, then management's role is limited: Hire the right people, and get out of their way. If it's largely the latter, management must play a more vigorous role: Establish the right roles and processes, set clear goals and relevant measures, and review progress at every step. Peter Drucker, with the masterly subtlety that is his trademark, comes down somewhere in the middle. Yes, he writes in this article, innovation is real work, and it can and should be managed like any other corporate function. But that doesn't mean it's the same as other business activities. Indeed, innovation is the work of knowing *rather than* doing.

Drucker argues that most innovative business ideas come from methodically analyzing seven areas of opportunity, some of which lie within particular companies or industries and some of which lie in broader social or demographic trends. Astute managers will ensure that their organizations maintain a clear focus on all seven. But analysis will take you only so far. Once you've identified an attractive opportunity, you still need a leap of imagination to arrive at the right response—call it "functional inspiration."

DESPITE MUCH DISCUSSION these days of the "entrepreneurial personality," few of the entrepreneurs with whom I have worked during the past 30 years had such personalities. But I have known many people— salespeople, surgeons, journalists, scholars, even musicians—who did have them without being the least bit entrepreneurial. What all the successful entrepreneurs I have met have in common is not a certain kind of personality but a commitment to the systematic practice of innovation.

Innovation is the specific function of entrepreneurship, whether in an existing business, a public service institution, or a new venture started by a lone individual in the family kitchen. It is the means by which the entrepreneur either creates new wealth-producing resources or endows existing resources with enhanced potential for creating wealth.

Today, much confusion exists about the proper definition of entrepreneurship. Some observers use the term to refer to all small businesses; others, to all new businesses. In practice, however, a great many well-established businesses engage in highly successful entrepreneurship. The term, then, refers not to an enterprise's size or age but to a certain kind of activity. At the heart of that activity is innovation: the effort to create purposeful, focused change in an enterprise's economic or social potential.

Sources of Innovation

There are, of course, innovations that spring from a flash of genius. Most innovations, however, especially the successful ones, result from a conscious, purposeful search for innovation opportunities, which are found only in a few situations. Four such areas of opportunity exist within a company or industry: unexpected occurrences, incongruities, process needs, and industry and market changes.

Three additional sources of opportunity exist outside a company in its social and intellectual environment: demographic changes, changes in perception, and new knowledge.

True, these sources overlap, different as they may be in the nature of their risk, difficulty, and complexity, and the potential for innovation may well lie in more than one area at a time. But together, they account for the great majority of all innovation opportunities.

1 UNEXPECTED OCCURRENCES

Consider, first, the easiest and simplest source of innovation opportunity: the unexpected. In the early 1930s, IBM developed the first modern accounting machine, which was designed for banks. But banks in 1933 did not buy new equipment. What saved the company—according to

a story that Thomas Watson, Sr., the company's founder
and long-term CEO, often told—was its exploitation of
an unexpected success: The New York Public Library
wanted to buy a machine. Unlike the banks, libraries in
those early New Deal days had money, and Watson sold
more than a hundred of his otherwise unsalable
machines to libraries.

Fifteen years later, when everyone believed that computers were designed for advanced scientific work, business unexpectedly showed an interest in a machine that
could do payroll. Univac, which had the most advanced
machine, spurned business applications. But IBM immediately realized it faced a possible unexpected success,
redesigned what was basically Univac's machine for such
mundane applications as payroll, and within five years
became a leader in the computer industry, a position it
has maintained to this day.

The unexpected failure may be an equally important
source of innovation opportunities. Everyone knows
about the Ford Edsel as the biggest new-car failure in automotive history. What very few people seem to know,
however, is that the Edsel's failure was the foundation for
much of the company's later success. Ford planned the
Edsel, the most carefully designed car to that point in
American automotive history, to give the company a full
product line with which to compete with General Motors.
When it bombed, despite all the planning, market research, and design that had gone into it, Ford realized
that something was happening in the automobile market
that ran counter to the basic assumptions on which GM
and everyone else had been designing and marketing cars.
No longer was the market segmented primarily by income
groups; the new principle of segmentation was what we
now call "lifestyles." Ford's response was the Mustang, a

car that gave the company a distinct personality and reestablished it as an industry leader.

Unexpected successes and failures are such productive sources of innovation opportunities because most businesses dismiss them, disregard them, and even resent them. The German scientist who around 1905 synthesized novocaine, the first nonaddictive narcotic, had intended it to be used in major surgical procedures like amputation. Surgeons, however, preferred total anesthesia for such procedures; they still do. Instead, novocaine found a ready appeal among dentists. Its inventor spent the remaining years of his life traveling from dental school to dental school making speeches that forbade dentists from "misusing" his noble invention in applications for which he had not intended it.

This is a caricature, to be sure, but it illustrates the attitude managers often take to the unexpected: "It should not have happened." Corporate reporting systems further ingrain this reaction, for they draw attention away from unanticipated possibilities. The typical monthly or quarterly report has on its first page a list of problems—that is, the areas where results fall short of expectations. Such information is needed, of course, to help prevent deterioration of performance. But it also suppresses the recognition of new opportunities. The first acknowledgment of a possible opportunity usually applies to an area in which a company does better than budgeted. Thus genuinely entrepreneurial businesses have two "first pages"—a problem page and an opportunity page—and managers spend equal time on both.

2 INCONGRUITIES

Alcon Laboratories was one of the success stories of the 1960s because Bill Conner, the company's cofounder, exploited an incongruity in medical technology. The cataract operation is the world's third or fourth most common surgical procedure. During the past 300 years, doctors systematized it to the point that the only "old-fashioned" step left was the cutting of a ligament. Eye surgeons had learned to cut the ligament with complete success, but it was so different a procedure from the rest of the operation, and so incompatible with it, that they often dreaded it. It was incongruous.

Doctors had known for 50 years about an enzyme that could dissolve the ligament without cutting. All Conner did was to add a preservative to this enzyme that gave it a few months' shelf life. Eye surgeons immediately accepted the new compound, and Alcon found itself with a worldwide monopoly. Fifteen years later, Nestlé bought the company for a fancy price.

Such an incongruity within the logic or rhythm of a process is only one possibility out of which innovation opportunities may arise. Another source is incongruity between economic realities. For instance, whenever an industry has a steadily growing market but falling profit margins—as, say, in the steel industries of developed countries between 1950 and 1970—an incongruity exists. The innovative response: minimills.

An incongruity between expectations and results can also open up possibilities for innovation. For 50 years after the turn of the century, shipbuilders and shipping companies worked hard both to make ships faster and to lower their fuel consumption. Even so, the more success-ful they were in boosting speed and trimming their fuel needs, the worse the economics of ocean freighters became. By 1950 or so, the ocean freighter was dying, if not already dead.

All that was wrong, however, was an incongruity between the industry's assumptions and its realities. The real costs did not come from doing work (that is, being at sea) but from *not* doing work (that is, sitting idle in port). Once managers understood where costs truly lay, the innovations were obvious: the roll-on and roll-off ship and the container ship. These solutions, which involved old technology, simply applied to the ocean freighter what railroads and truckers had been using for 30 years. A shift in viewpoint, not in technology, totally changed the economics of ocean shipping and turned it into one of the major growth industries of the last 20 to 30 years.

3 PROCESS NEEDS

Anyone who has ever driven in Japan knows that the country has no modern highway system. Its roads still follow the paths laid down for—or by—oxcarts in the tenth century. What makes the system work for automobiles and trucks is an adaptation of the reflector used on American highways since the early 1930s. The reflector lets each car see which other cars are approaching from any one of a half-dozen directions. This minor invention, which enables traffic to move smoothly and with a minimum of accidents, exploited a process need.

What we now call the media had its origin in two innovations developed around 1890 in response to process needs. One was Ottmar Mergenthaler's Linotype, which made it possible to produce newspapers quickly and in large volume. The other was a social innovation, modern advertising, invented by the first true newspaper publishers, Adolph Ochs of the *New York Times*, Joseph Pulitzer of the *New York World*, and William Randolph Hearst. Advertising made it possible for them to distribute news practically free of charge, with the profit coming from marketing.

4 INDUSTRY AND MARKET CHANGES

Managers may believe that industry structures are ordained by the good Lord, but these structures can—and often do—change overnight. Such change creates tremendous opportunity for innovation.

One of American business's great success stories in recent decades is the brokerage firm of Donaldson, Lufkin & Jenrette, recently acquired by the Equitable Life Assurance Society. DL&J was founded in 1960 by three young men, all graduates of the Harvard Business School, who realized that the structure of the financial industry was changing as institutional investors became dominant. These young men had practically no capital and no connections. Still, within a few years, their firm had become a leader in the move to negotiated commissions and one of Wall Street's stellar performers. It was the first to be incorporated and go public.

In a similar fashion, changes in industry structure have created massive innovation opportunities for American health care providers. During the past ten or 15 years, independent surgical and psychiatric clinics, emergency centers, and HMOs have opened throughout the country. Comparable opportunities in telecommunications followed industry upheavals—in transmission (with the emergence of MCI and Sprint in long-distance service) and in equipment (with the emergence of such companies as Rolm in the manufacturing of private branch exchanges).

When an industry grows quickly—the critical figure seems to be in the neighborhood of 40% growth in ten years or less—its structure changes. Established companies, concentrating on defending what they already have, tend not to counterattack when a newcomer challenges them. Indeed, when market or industry structures change, traditional industry leaders again and again neglect the fastest growing market segments. New opportunities rarely fit the way the industry has always approached the market, defined it, or organized to serve it. Innovators therefore have a good chance of being left alone for a long time.

5 DEMOGRAPHIC CHANGES

Of the outside sources of innovation opportunities, demographics are the most reliable. Demographic events have known lead times; for instance, every person who will be in the American labor force by the year 2000 has already been born. Yet because policy makers often neglect demographics, those who watch them and exploit them can reap great rewards.

The Japanese are ahead in robotics because they paid attention to demographics. Everyone in the developed countries around 1970 or so knew that there was both a baby bust and an education explosion going on; about half or more of the young people were staying in school beyond high school. Consequently, the number of people available for traditional blue-collar work in manufacturing was bound to decrease and become inadequate by 1990. Everyone knew this, but only the Japanese acted on it, and they now have a ten-year lead in robotics.

Much the same is true of Club Mediterranee's success in the travel and resort business. By 1970, thoughtful observers could have seen the emergence of large numbers of affluent and educated young adults in Europe and the United States. Not comfortable with the kind of vacations their working-class parents had enjoyed—the summer weeks at Brighton or Atlantic City—these young people were ideal customers for a new and exotic version of the "hangout" of their teen years.

Managers have known for a long time that demographics matter, but they have always believed that population statistics change slowly. In this century, however, they don't. Indeed, the innovation opportunities made possible by changes in the numbers of people—and in their age distribution, education, occupations, and geographic location—are among the most rewarding and least risky of entrepreneurial pursuits.

6 CHANGES IN PERCEPTION

"The glass is half full" and "The glass is half empty" are descriptions of the same phenomenon but have vastly different meanings. Changing a manager's perception of a glass from half full to half empty opens up big innovation opportunities.

All factual evidence indicates, for instance, that in the last 20 years, Americans' health has improved with unprecedented speed—whether measured by mortality rates for the newborn, survival rates for the very old, the incidence of cancers (other than lung cancer), cancer cure rates, or other factors. Even so, collective hypochondria grips the nation. Never before has there been so much concern with or fear about health. Suddenly, everything seems to cause cancer or degenerative heart disease or premature loss of memory. The glass is clearly half empty.

Rather than rejoicing in great improvements in health, Americans seem to be emphasizing how far away they still are from immortality. This view of things has created many opportunities for innovations: markets for new health care magazines, for exercise classes and jogging equipment, and for all kinds of health foods. The fastest growing new U.S. business in 1983 was a company that makes indoor exercise equipment.

A change in perception does not alter facts. It changes their meaning, though—and very quickly. It took less than two years for the computer to change from being perceived as a threat and as something only big businesses would use to something one buys for doing income tax. Economics do not necessarily dictate such a change; in fact, they may be irrelevant. What determines whether people see a glass as half full or half empty is mood rather than fact, and a change in mood often defies quantification. But it is not exotic. It is concrete. It can be defined. It can be tested. And it can be exploited for innovation opportunity.

Knowledge-based innovations can be temperamental, capricious, and hard to direct.

7 NEW KNOWLEDGE

Among history-making innovations, those that are based on new knowledge—whether scientific, technical, or social—rank high. They are the superstars of entrepreneurship; they get the publicity and the money. They are what people usually mean when they talk of innovation, although not all innovations based on knowledge are important.

Knowledge-based innovations differ from all others in the time they take, in their casualty rates, and in their predictability, as well as in the challenges they pose to entrepreneurs. Like most superstars, they can be temperamental, capricious, and hard to direct. They have, for instance, the longest lead time of all innovations. There is a protracted span between the emergence of new knowledge and its distillation into usable technology. Then there is another long period before this new technology appears in the marketplace in products, processes, or services. Overall, the lead time involved is something like 50 years, a figure that has not shortened appreciably throughout history.

To become effective, innovation of this sort usually demands not one kind of knowledge but many. Consider one of the most potent knowledge-based innovations: modern banking. The theory of the entrepreneurial bank—that is, of the purposeful use of capital to generate economic development—was formulated by the Comte de Saint-Simon during the era of Napoleon. Despite Saint-Simon's extraordinary prominence, it was not until 30 years after his death in 1825 that two of his disciples, the brothers Jacob and Isaac Pereire, established the first entrepreneurial bank, the Credit Mobilier, and ushered in what we now call finance capitalism.

The Pereires, however, did not know modern commercial banking, which developed at about the same time across the channel in England. The Credit Mobilier failed ignominiously. A few years later, two young men— one an American, J.P. Morgan, and one a German, Georg Siemens—put together the French theory of entrepreneurial banking and the English theory of commercial banking to create the first successful modern banks: J.P. Morgan & Company in New York, and the Deutsche Bank in Berlin. Ten years later, a young Japanese, Shibusawa Eiichi, adapted Siemens's concept to his country and thereby laid the foundation of Japan's modern economy. This is how knowledge-based innovation always works.

The computer, to cite another example, required no fewer than six separate strands of knowledge:

- binary arithmetic;

- Charles Babbage's conception of a calculating machine, in the first half of the nineteenth century;

- the punch card, invented by Herman Hollerith for the U.S. census of 1890;

- the audion tube, an electronic switch invented in 1906;

- symbolic logic, which was developed between 1910 and 1913 by Bertrand Russell and Alfred North Whitehead;

- and concepts of programming and feedback that came out of abortive attempts during World War I to develop effective antiaircraft guns.

Although all the necessary knowledge was available by 1918, the first operational digital computer did not appear until 1946.

Long lead times and the need for convergence among different kinds of knowledge explain the peculiar rhythm of knowledge-based innovation, its attractions, and its dangers. During a long gestation period, there is a lot of talk and little action. Then, when all the elements suddenly converge, there is tremendous excitement and activity and an enormous amount of speculation. Between 1880 and 1890, for example, almost 1,000 electric-apparatus companies were founded in developed countries. Then, as always, there was a crash and a shake-out. By 1914, only 25 were still alive. In the early 1920s, 300 to 500 automobile companies existed in the United States; by 1960, only four of them remained.

It may be difficult, but knowledge-based innovation can be managed. Success requires careful analysis of the various kinds of knowledge needed to make an innovation possible. Both J.P. Morgan and Georg Siemens did this when they established their banking ventures. The Wright brothers did this when they developed the first operational airplane.

Careful analysis of the needs—and, above all, the capabilities—of the intended user is also essential. It may seem paradoxical, but knowledge-based innovation is more market dependent than any other kind of innovation. De Havilland, a British company, designed and built the first passenger jet, but it did not analyze what the market needed and therefore did not identify two key factors. One was configuration—that is, the right size with the right payload for the routes on which a jet would give an airline the greatest advantage. The other was equally mundane: How could the airlines finance the purchase of such an expensive plane? Because de Havilland failed to do an adequate user analysis, two American companies, Boeing and Douglas, took over the commercial jet-aircraft industry.

Principles of Innovation

Purposeful, systematic innovation begins with the analysis of the sources of new opportunities. Depending on the context, sources will have different importance at different times. Demographics, for instance, may be of little concern to innovators of fundamental industrial processes like steelmaking, although the Linotype machine became successful primarily because there were not enough skilled typesetters available to satisfy a mass market. By the same token, new knowledge may be of little relevance to someone innovating a social instrument to satisfy a need that changing demographics or tax laws have created. But whatever the situation, innovators must analyze all opportunity sources.

Because innovation is both conceptual and perceptual, would-be innovators must also go out and look, ask, and listen. Successful innovators use both the right and left sides of their brains. They work out analytically what the innovation has to be to satisfy an opportunity. Then they go out and look at potential users to study their expectations, their values, and their needs.

To be effective, an innovation has to be simple, and it has to be focused. It should do only one thing; otherwise it confuses people. Indeed, the greatest praise an innovation can receive is for people to say, "This is obvious! Why didn't I think of it? It's so simple!" Even the innovation that creates new users and new markets should be directed toward a specific, clear, and carefully designed application.

Effective innovations start small. They are not grandiose. It may be to enable a moving vehicle to draw electric power while it runs along rails, the innovation that made possible the electric streetcar. Or it may be the elementary idea of putting the same number of matches into a matchbox (it used to be 50). This simple notion made possible the automatic filling of matchboxes and gave the Swedes a world monopoly on matches for half a century. By contrast, grandiose ideas for things that will "revolutionize an industry" are unlikely to work.

Innovation requires knowledge, ingenuity, and, above all else, focus.

In fact, no one can foretell whether a given innovation will end up a big business or a modest achievement. But even if the results are modest, the successful innovation aims from the beginning to become the standard setter, to determine the direction of a new technology or a new industry, to create the business that is—and remains—ahead of the pack. If an innovation does not aim at leadership from the beginning, it is unlikely to be innovative enough.

Above all, innovation is work rather than genius. It requires knowledge. It often requires ingenuity. And it requires focus. There are clearly people who are more talented innovators than others, but their talents lie in well-defined areas. Indeed, innovators rarely work in more than one area. For all his systematic innovative accomplishments, Thomas Edison worked only in the electrical field. An innovator in financial areas, Citibank for example, is not likely to embark on innovations in health care.

In innovation, as in any other endeavor, there is talent, there is ingenuity, and there is knowledge. But when all is said and done, what innovation requires is hard, focused, purposeful work. If diligence, persistence, and commitment are lacking, talent, ingenuity, and knowledge are of no avail.

There is, of course, far more to entrepreneurship than systematic innovation—distinct entrepreneurial strategies, for example, and the principles of entrepreneurial management, which are needed equally in the established enterprise, the public service organization, and the new venture. But the very foundation of entrepreneurship is the practice of systematic innovation.

Originally published in August 2002
Reprint R0208F

Research That Reinvents the Corporation

JOHN SEELY BROWN

Executive Summary

AS COMPANIES TRY TO KEEP pace with rapid changes in technology and cope with unstable business environments, their research departments have to do more than simply invent new products. They must design the new technological and organizational architectures that make a continuously innovating company possible.

In this 1991 article, John Seely Brown, then director of Xerox's Palo Alto Research Center (PARC), describes the business logic behind this distinctive vision of research's role and the ways Xerox PARC tried to realize that vision. Its researcher developed prototypes of new work practices as well as new technologies and products. They designed new uses for technology to encourage the local innovation that, they found, occurs naturally at all levels of any big company. And they experimented with new techniques for what the author terms "coproducing" technological and organizational innovations with Xerox's customers.

Xerox's business is technology, but Seely Brown argues that any company, no matter what its business, must eventually grapple with the issues he raises. The successful company of the future must understand how people really work and must adapt its technology to the work rather than the other way around. It must know how to create an environment that allows for continuous innovation by all employees. It must rethink traditional business assumptions and tap into needs that customers don't even know they have. In essence, he argues, the most important invention that will come out of the corporate research lab in the future will be the corporation itself.

The locus of corporate innovation has traditionally been product development. But in times of rapid and unpredictable change, the creation of individual products becomes less important than the creation of a general organizational aptitude for innovation. That's the central message of John Seely Brown's groundbreaking article "Research That Reinvents the Corporation."

Seely Brown offers a new vision for the corporate research function: Rather than focusing narrowly on developing technologies and products, R&D needs to broaden its agenda, helping companies invent new practices and processes that enhance their overall ingenuity and flexibility. Drawing on the experience of Xerox PARC—both its successes and its failures—Seely Brown offers four suggestions that are at once practical and transformative. He aims his advice at research depart-

ments, but it is equally valuable for any manager looking to build a continuously innovating organization.

THE MOST IMPORTANT INVENTION that will come out of the corporate research lab in the future will be the corporation itself. As companies try to keep pace with rapid changes in technology and cope with increasingly unstable business environments, the research department has to do more than simply innovate new products. It must design the new technological and organizational architectures that make possible a continuously innovating company. Put another way, corporate research must reinvent innovation.

At the Xerox Palo Alto Research Center (PARC) we've learned this lesson, at times, the hard way. Xerox created PARC in 1970 to pursue advanced research in computer science, electronics, and materials science. Over the next decade, PARC researchers were responsible for some of the basic innovations of the personal computer revolution—only to see other companies commercialize these innovations more quickly than Xerox. (See "PARC: Seedbed of the Computer Revolution" at the end of this article.) In the process, Xerox gained a reputation for fumbling the future and PARC for doing brilliant research but in isolation from the company's business.

That view is one-sided because it ignores the way that PARC innovations *have* paid off over the past 20 years. Still, it raises fundamental questions that many companies besides Xerox have been struggling with in recent years: What is the role of corporate research in a business environment characterized by tougher competition and nonstop technological change? And how can large companies better assimilate the latest innovations and quickly incorporate them in new products?

One popular answer to these questions is to shift the focus of the research department away from radical breakthroughs toward incremental innovation, away from basic research toward applied research. At PARC, we have chosen a different approach, one that cuts across both of these categories and combines the most useful features of each. We call it "pioneering research."

Like the best applied research, pioneering research is closely connected to the company's most pressing business problems. But like the best basic research, it seeks to redefine these problems fundamentally in order to come up with fresh—and sometimes radical—solutions. Our emphasis on pioneering research has led us to redefine what we mean by technology, by innovation, and, indeed, by research itself. Here are some of the new principles that we have identified.

1. Research on new work practices is as important as research on new products. Corporate research is traditionally viewed as the source of new technologies and products. At PARC, we believe it is equally important for research to invent new prototypes of organizational practice. This means going beyond the typical view of technology as an artifact—hardware and software—to explore its potential for creating new and more effective ways of working, what we call studying technology in use. Such activities are essential for companies to exploit successfully the next great breakthrough in information technology—"ubiquitous computing": the incorporation of information technology into a broad range of everyday objects.

2. Innovation is everywhere; the problem is learning from it. When corporate research begins to focus on a company's practice as well as its products, another principle quickly becomes clear: Innovation isn't the privileged activity of the research department. It goes on at all levels of a company—wherever employees confront problems, deal with unforeseen contingencies, or work their way around breakdowns in normal procedures. The problem is, few companies know how to learn from this local innovation and how to use it to improve their overall effectiveness. At PARC, we are studying this process of local innovation with employees on the front lines of Xerox's business and developing technologies to harvest its lessons for the company as a whole. By doing so, we hope to turn company size, so often seen as an obstacle to innovation, into an advantage—a rich seedbed of fresh insights about technology and new work practices.

3. Research can't just produce innovation; it must "coproduce" it. Before a company can learn from the innovation in its midst, it must rethink the process by which innovation is transmitted throughout the organization. Research must coproduce new technologies and work practices by developing with partners throughout the organization a shared understanding of why these innovations are important. On the one hand, that means challenging the outmoded background assumptions that so often distort the way people see new technologies, new market opportunities, and the entire business. On the other, it requires creating new ways to communicate the significance of radical innovations. Essentially, corporate research must prototype new mental models of the organization and its business.

4. The research department's ultimate innovation partner is the customer. Prototyping technology in use, harvesting local innovation, coproducing new mental models of the organization—all these activities that we are pursuing inside Xerox are directly applicable to our customers as well. In fact, our future competitive advantage will not just depend on selling information technology products to customers. It will depend on coproducing these products with customers—customizing technology and work practices to meet their current and future needs. One role of corporate research in this activity is to invent methods and tools to help customers identify their latent needs and improve their own capacity for continuous innovation.

At PARC, we've only begun to explore the implications of these new principles. Our activities in each of these areas are little more than interesting experiments. Still, we have defined a promising and exciting new direction. Without giving up our strong focus on state-of-the-art information technologies, we are also studying the human and organizational barriers to innovation. And using the entire Xerox organization as our laboratory, we are experimenting with new techniques for helping people grasp the revolutionary potential of new technologies and work practices.

The result: important contributions to Xerox's core products but also a distinctive approach to innovation with implications far beyond our company. Our business happens to be technology, but any company—no matter what the business—must eventually grapple with the issues we've been addressing. The successful company of the future must understand how people really work and how technology can help them work more effectively. It must know how to create an environment for continual innovation on the part of all employees. It must rethink traditional business assumptions and tap needs that customers don't even know they have yet. It must use research to reinvent the corporation.

Technology Gets Out of the Way

At the foundation of our new approach to research is a particular vision of technology. As the cost of computing power continues to plummet, two things become possible. First, more and more electronic technology will be incorporated in everyday office devices. Second, increased computing power will allow users to tailor the technology to meet their specific needs.

Together these trends lead to a paradoxical result. When information technology is everywhere and can be customized to match more closely the work to be done, the technology itself will become invisible. The next great breakthrough of the information age will be the disappearance of discrete information-technology products. Technology is finally becoming powerful enough to get out of the way.

Consider the example of the photocopier. Ever since Chester Carlson first invented xerography some 50 years ago, the technology of photocopiers has been more or less the same. In a process somewhat similar to photography, a light-lens projects an image of the page onto a photoreceptor. The image is then developed with a dry toner to produce the copy. But information technology is transforming the copier with implications as radical as those accompanying the invention of xerography itself.

Today our copiers are complex computing and communications devices. Inside Xerox's high-end machines are some 30 microprocessors linked together by local area networks. They continuously monitor the operations of the machine and make adjustments to compensate for wear and tear, thus increasing reliability and ensuring consistent, high copy quality. Information systems inside our copiers also make the machines easier to use by constantly providing users with information linked to the specific tasks they are performing. (See "How Xerox Redesigned Its Copiers" at the end of this article.) These innovations were crucial to Xerox's success in meeting Japanese competition and regaining market share during the past decade.

But these changes are only the beginning. Once copiers become computing devices, they also become sensors that collect information about their own performance that can be used to improve service and product design. For example, Xerox recently introduced a new standard feature on our high-end copiers known as "remote interactive communication" or RIC. RIC is an expert system inside the copier that monitors the information technology controlling the machine and, using some artificial-intelligence techniques, predicts when the machine will next break down. Once RIC predicts a breakdown will occur, it automatically places a call to a branch office and downloads its prediction, along with its reasoning. A computer at the branch office does some further analysis and schedules a repair person to visit the site *before* the expected time of failure.

For the customer, RIC means never having to see the machine fail. For Xerox, it means not only providing better service but also having a new way to listen to our customer. As RIC collects information on the performance of our copiers—in real-world business environments, year in and year out—we will eventually be able to use that information to guide how we design future generations of copiers.

RIC is one example of how information technology invisible to the user is transforming the copier. But the ultimate conclusion of this technological transformation is the disappearance of the copier as a stand-alone device. Recently, Xerox introduced its most versatile office machine ever—a product that replaces traditional light-lens copying techniques with digital copying, where documents are electronically scanned to create an image stored in a computer, then printed out whenever needed. In the future, digital copiers will allow the user to scan a document at one site and print it out somewhere else—much like a fax. And once it scans a document, a copier will be able to store, edit, or enhance the document—like a computer file—before printing it. When this happens, the traditional distinction between the copier and other office devices like computers, printers, and fax machines will disappear—leaving a flexible, multifunctional device able to serve a variety of user needs.

What is happening to the copier will eventually happen to all office devices. As computing power becomes ubiquitous—incorporated not only in copiers but also in filing cabinets, desktops, white boards, even electronic "Post-it Notes"—it will become more and more invisible, a taken-for-granted part of any work environment, much as books, reports, or other documents are today. What's more, increased computing power will make possible new uses of information technology that are far more flexible than current systems. In effect, technology will become so flexible that users will be able to customize it ever more precisely to meet their particular needs—a process that might be termed "mass customization."

We are already beginning to see this development in software design. Increased computing power is making possible new approaches to writing software such as object-oriented programming (developed at PARC in the 1970s). This technique makes it easier for users to perform customizing tasks that previously required a trained programmer and allows them to adapt and redesign information systems as their needs change. From a purely technical perspective, object-oriented programming may be less efficient than traditional programming techniques. But the flexibility it makes possible is far more suited to the needs of constantly evolving organizations.

Indeed, at some point in the not-too-distant future—certainly within the next decade—information technology will become a kind of generic entity, almost like clay. And the "product" will not exist until it enters a specific situation, where vendor and customer will mold it to the work practices of the customer organization. When that happens, information technology as a distinct category of products will become invisible. It will dissolve into the work itself. And companies like ours might sell not products but rather the expertise to help users define their needs and create the products best suited to them. Our product will be our customers' learning.

Harvesting Local Innovation

The trend toward ubiquitous computing and mass customization is made possible by technology. The emphasis, however, is not on the technology itself but on the work practices it supports. In the future, organizations won't have to shape how they work to fit the narrow confines of an inflexible technology. Rather, they can begin to design information systems to support the way people really work.

That's why some of the most important research at PARC in the past decade has been done by anthropologists. They have studied occupations and work practices throughout the company—clerks in an accounts-payable office who issue checks to suppliers, technical representatives who repair copying machines, designers who develop new products, even novice users of Xerox's copiers. This research has produced fundamental insights into the nature of innovation, organizational learning, and good product design.

We got involved in the anthropology of work for a good business reason. We figured that before we went ahead and applied technology to work, we had better have a clear understanding of exactly how people do their jobs. Most people assume—we did too, at first—that the formal procedures defining a job, or the explicit structure of an organizational chart, accurately describe what employees do, especially in highly routinized occupations. But when PARC anthropologist Lucy Suchman began studying Xerox accounting clerks in 1979, she uncovered an unexpected and intriguing contradiction.

When Suchman asked the clerks how they did their jobs, their descriptions corresponded more or less to the formal procedures of the job manual. But when she observed them at work, she discovered that the clerks weren't really following those procedures at all. Instead, they relied on a rich variety of informal practices that weren't in any manual but turned out to be crucial to getting the work done. In fact, the clerks were constantly improvising, inventing new methods to deal with unexpected difficulties and solve immediate problems. Without being aware of it, they were far more innovative and creative than anybody who heard them describe their "routine" jobs ever would have thought.

Unfortunately, it's the rare company that understands the importance of informal improvisation, let along respects it as a legitimate business activity.

Suchman concluded that formal office procedures have almost nothing to do with how people do their jobs. People use procedures to understand the goals of a particular job—for example, what kind of information a particular file has to contain in order for a bill to be paid—not to identify the steps to take to get from here to there. But to reach that goal—actually collecting and verifying the information and making sure the bill is paid—people constantly invent new work practices to cope with the unforeseen contingencies of the moment. These informal activities remain mostly invisible, since they do not fall within the normal, specified procedures that employees are expected to follow or managers expect to see. But these work arounds enable an all-important flexibility that allows organizations to cope with the unexpected, as well as to profit from experience and to change.

If local innovation is as important and pervasive as we suspect, then big companies have the potential to be remarkably innovative—if they can somehow capture this innovation and learn from it. Unfortunately, it's the rare company that understands the importance of informal improvisation, let alone respects it as a legitimate business activity. In most cases, ideas generated by employees in the course of their work are lost to the organization as a whole. An individual might use them to make his or her job easier and perhaps even share them informally with a small group of colleagues. But such informal insights about work rarely spread beyond the local work group. And because most information systems are based on the formal procedures of work, not the informal practices crucial to getting it done, they often tend to make things worse rather than better. As a result, this important source of organizational learning is either ignored or suppressed.

At PARC, we are trying to design new uses of technology that leverage the incremental innovation coming from within the entire company. We want to create work environments where people can legitimately improvise and where those improvisations can be captured and made part of the organization's collective knowledge base.

One way is to provide people with easy-to-use programming tools so they can customize the information systems and computer applications that they work with. To take a small example, my assistant is continually discovering new ways to improve the work systems in our office. She has more ideas for perfecting, say, our electronic calendar system than any researcher does. After all, she uses it every day and frequently bumps up against its limitations. So instead of designing a new and better calendar system, we created a programming language known as CUSP (for customized user system program) that allows users to modify the system themselves.

We've taken another small step in this direction at EuroPARC, our European research lab in Cambridge, England. Researchers there have invented an even more-advanced software system known as Buttons—bits of computer code structured and packaged so that even people without a lot of training in computers can modify them. With Buttons, secretaries, clerks, technicians, and others can create their own software applications, send them to colleagues throughout the corporation over our electronic mail network, and adapt any Buttons they receive from others to their own needs. Through the use of such tools, we are translating local innovation into software that can be easily disseminated and used by all.

New technologies can also serve as powerful aids for organizational learning. For example, in 1984, Xerox's service organization asked us to research ways to improve the effectiveness of its training programs. Training the company's 14,500 service technicians who repair copying machines is extremely costly and time consuming. What's more, the time it takes to train the service workforce on a new technology is key to how fast the company can launch new products.

The service organization was hoping we could make traditional classroom training happen faster, perhaps by creating some kind of expert system. But based on our evolving theory of work and innovation, we decided to take another approach. We sent out a former service technician, who had since gone on to do graduate work in anthropology, to find out how reps actually do their jobs—not what they or their managers say they do but what they really do and how they learn the skills that they actually use. He took the company training program, actually worked on repair jobs in the field, and interviewed tech reps about their jobs. He concluded that the reps learn the most not from formal training courses but out in the field—by working on real problems and discussing them informally with colleagues. Indeed, the stories tech reps tell one another—around the coffeepot, in the lunchroom, or while working together on a particularly difficult problem—are crucial to continuous learning.

In a sense, these stories are the real "expert systems" used by tech reps on the job. They are a storehouse of past problems and diagnoses, a template for constructing a theory about the current problem, and the basis for making an educated stab at a solution. By creating such stories and constantly refining them through conversations with each other, tech reps are creating a powerful organizational memory that is a valuable resource for the company.

As a result of this research, we are rethinking the design of tech rep training—and the tech rep job itself—in terms of lifelong learning. How might a company support and leverage the storytelling that is crucial to building the expertise not only of individual tech reps but also of the entire tech rep community? And is there any way to link that expertise to other groups in the company who would benefit from it—for example, the designers who are creating the future generations of our systems?

One possibility is to create advanced multimedia information systems that would make it easier for reps and other employees to plug in to this collective social mind. Such a system might allow the reps to pass around annotated video clips of useful stories, much as scientists distribute their scientific papers, to sites all over the world. By commenting on one another's experiences, reps could refine and disseminate new knowledge. This distributed collective memory, containing all the informal expertise and lore of the occupation, could help tech reps—and the company—improve their capacity to learn from successes and failures.

Coproducing Innovation

Our approach to the issue of tech rep training is a good example of what we mean by pioneering research. We started with a real business problem, recognized by everyone, then reframed the problem to come up with solutions that no one had considered before. But this raises another challenge of pioneering research: how to communicate fresh insights

It's never enough to just tell people about some new insight. Rather, you have to get them to experience it in a way that evokes its power and possibility.

about familiar problems so that others can grasp their significance.

The traditional approach to communicating new innovations—a process that usually goes by the name of "technology transfer"—is to treat it as a simple problem of transferring information. Research has to pour new knowledge into people's heads like water from a pitcher into a glass. That kind of communication might work for incremental innovations. But when it comes to pioneering research that fundamentally redefines a technology, product, work process, or business problem, this approach doesn't work.

Instead of pouring knowledge into people's heads, you need to help them grind a new set of eyeglasses so they can see the world in a new way.

It's never enough to just *tell* people about some new insight. Rather, you have to get them to experience it in a way that evokes its power and possibility. Instead of pouring knowledge into people's heads, you need to help them grind a new set of eyeglasses so they can see the world in a new way. That involves challenging the implicit assumptions that have shaped the way people in an organization have historically looked at things. It also requires creating new communication techniques that actually get people to experience the implications of an innovation.

To get an idea of this process, consider the strategic implications of digital copying for a company like Xerox. Xerox owes its existence to a particular technology— light-lens xerography. That tradition has shaped how the company conceives of products, markets, and customer needs, often in ways that are not so easy to identify. But digital copying renders many of those assumptions obsolete. Therefore, making these assumptions explicit and analyzing their limitations is an essential strategic task.

Until recently, most people at Xerox thought of information technology primarily as a way to make traditional copiers cheaper and better. They didn't realize that digital copying would transform the business, with broad implications not just for copiers but also for office information systems in general. Working with the Xerox corporate strategy office, we've tried to find a way to open up the corporate imagination—to get people to move beyond the standard ways they thought about copiers.

One approach we took a couple of years ago was to create a video for top management, which we called the "unfinished document." In the video, researchers at PARC who knew the technology extremely well discussed the potential of digital copying to transform people's work. But they didn't just talk about it; they actually acted it out in skits. They created mock-ups of the technology and then simulated how it might affect different work activities. They attempted to portray not just the technology but also the technology in use.

We thought of the unfinished document as a conceptual-envisioning experiment—an attempt to imagine how a technology might be used before we started building it. We showed the video to some top corporate officers to get their intuitional juices flowing. The document was unfinished in the sense

By learning how the corporation rejects certain ideas, we hope to uncover those features of the corporate culture that need to change.

that the whole point of the exercise was to get the viewers to complete the video by suggesting their own ideas for how they might use the new technology and what these new uses might mean for the business. In the process, they weren't just learning about a new technology; they were creating a new mental model of the business.

Senior management is an important partner for research, but our experiments at coproduction aren't limited to the top. We are also involved in initiatives to get managers far down in the organization to reflect on the obstacles blocking innovation in the Xerox culture. For example, one project takes as its starting point the familiar fact that the best innovations are often the product of "renegades" on the periphery of the company. PARC researchers are part of a company group that is trying to understand why this is so often the case. We are studying some of the company's most adventuresome product development programs to learn how the larger Xerox organization can sometimes obstruct a new product or work process. By learning how the corporation rejects certain ideas, we hope to uncover those features of the corporate culture that need to change.

Such efforts are the beginning of what we hope will become an ongoing dialogue in the company about Xerox's organizational practice. By challenging the background assumptions that traditionally stifle innovation, we hope to create an environment where the creativity of talented people can flourish and pull new ideas into the business.

Innovating with the Customer

Finally, research's ultimate partner in coproduction is the customer. The logical end point of all the activities I have described is for corporate research to move outside the company and work with customers to coproduce the technology and work systems they will need in the future.

It is important to distinguish this activity from conventional market research. Most market research assumes either that a particular product already exists or that customers already know what they need. At PARC, we are focusing on systems that do not yet exist and on needs that are not yet clearly defined. We want to help customers become aware of their latent needs, then customize systems to meet them. Put another way, we are trying to prototype a need or use before we prototype a system.

One step in this direction is an initiative of Xerox's Corporate Research Group (of which PARC is a part) known as the Express project. Express is an experiment in product delivery management designed to commercialize PARC technologies more rapidly by directly involving customers in the innovation process. Based at PARC, the project brings together employees from one of our customers (the Palo Alto–based pharmaceutical company Syntex) with a small team of Xerox researchers, engineers, and marketers into a single organization.

Syntex's more than 1,000 researchers do R&D on new drugs up for approval by the Food and Drug Administration. The Express team is exploring ways to use core technologies developed at PARC to help the pharmaceutical company manage the more than 300,000 case-report forms it collects each year. (The forms report on tests of new drugs on human volunteers.) Syntex employees have spent time at PARC learning our technologies in progress. Similarly, the members of the team from Xerox have intensively studied Syntex's work processes—much as PARC anthropologists have studied work inside our own company.

Once the project team defined the pharmaceutical company's key business needs and the PARC technologies that could be used to meet them, programmers from both companies worked together to create some prototypes. One new system, for example, is known as the Forms Receptionist. It combines technologies for document recognition, document interchange and translation, and intelligent scanning to scan, sort, file, and distribute Syntex's case reports. For Syntex, the new system solves an important business problem. For Xerox, it is the prototype of a product that we eventually hope to offer to other customers in the entire pharmaceutical industry.

We are also treating Express as a case study in coproduction, worth investigating in its own right. The Express team has videotaped all the interactions between Xerox and Syntex employees, and developed a computerized index to guide the team through this visual database. And a second research team is conducting an in-depth study of the entire Xerox-Syntex collaboration. By studying the project, we hope to learn valuable lessons about coproduction.

One of the most interesting lessons we've learned from the Express project so far is just how long it takes to create a shared understanding among the members of such product teams—a common language, a sense of purpose, and a definition of goals. This is similar to the experience of many interfunctional teams, which end up reproducing inside the team the same conflicting perspectives the teams were designed to overcome in the first place. We believe that the persistence of such misunderstandings may be a serious drag on product development.

Thus a critical task for the future is to explore how information technology might be used to accelerate the creation of mutual understandings within work groups. The ultimate goal of this process would be to build what might be called an "envisioning laboratory"—a powerful computer environment where Xerox customers would have access to advanced programming tools that they could use to quickly model and envision the consequences of new systems. Working with Xerox's development and marketing organizations, customers could try out new system configurations, reflect on the appropriateness of the systems for their business, and progressively refine and tailor them to match their business needs. Such an environment would be a new kind of technological medium. Its purpose would be to create evocative simulations of new systems and new products before actually building them.

The envisioning laboratory does not yet exist. Still, it is not so far-fetched to imagine a point in the near future when major corporations will have research centers with the technological capability of, say, a multimedia computer-animation studio like Lucasfilm. Using state-of-the-art animation techniques, such a laboratory could create elaborate simulations of new products and use them to explore the implications of those products on a customer's work organization. Prototypes that today take years to create could be roughed out in a matter of weeks or days.

When this happens, phrases like "continuous innovation" and the "customer-driven" company will take on new meaning. And the transformation of corporate research—and the corporation as a whole—will be complete.

PARC: Seedbed of the Computer Revolution

FORMER XEROX CEO C. Peter McColough created the Palo Alto Research Center (PARC) in 1970 to perform basic research in computing and electronics and to study what McColough called "the architecture of information"—how complex organizations use information. PARC hired some of the best computer scientists in the world and gave them virtually unlimited funding to pursue their ideas.

The scientific payoff from PARC was immediate. Throughout the 1970s, PARC researchers produced a series of fundamental innovations in computer technology that would prove to be the building blocks of the personal computer revolution: bit-map display computer screens that make easy-to-use graphic interfaces possible, local area networks for distributed computing, overlapping screen windows, point-and-click editing using a mouse, and Smalltalk, the first object-oriented programming language.

Xerox never became a dominant player in the personal computer industry. But PARC's research has nevertheless directly fed the company's strategic businesses. PARC developed the first prototype of laser printing in 1973. By 1990, laser printing was a several-billion-dollar business at Xerox. And PARC's innovations in local area networks and its distinctive computer interface designs have been successfully incorporated into Xerox copiers and printers, an innovation that was crucial to the company's successfully meeting the challenge from Japanese competition in the 1980s.

Whereas PARC scientists of the 1970s had a technical vision, today the center is increasingly focusing on the interrelationships between technology and work. In 1990, anthropologists, sociologists, linguists, and psychologists complement PARC's traditional research staff of computer scientists, physicists, and engineers. And much of the center's computer science research emphasizes how information technology can be used to support effective group collaboration—a field known as "computer-supported cooperative work."

–Robert Howard

How Xerox Redesigned Its Copiers

IN THE EARLY 1980S, Xerox's copier business faced a big problem. Service calls were increasing, and more and more customers were reporting that our newest copiers were unreliable. The complaints couldn't have come at a worse time. We had been late to recognize market opportunities for low- and midrange copiers, and Japanese competitors like Canon were cutting into our market share. Now Xerox's reputation for quality was at stake.

After interviewing some customers, we discovered that unreliability was not the real problem. Our copiers weren't breaking down more frequently than before; in fact, many of the service calls were unnecessary. But customers were finding the copiers increasingly difficult to use. Because they couldn't get their work done, they perceived the machines as unreliable.

The source of the problem was our copier design. Traditionally, Xerox technology designers—like most engineers—have striven to make machines idiot proof. The idea was to foresee all the possible things that could go wrong, then either design them out of the system or provide detailed instructions of what to do should they occur.

But as we kept adding new functions, we had to add more and more information, usually stored on flip cards attached to the machine. The copiers became so complex that it was harder for the new user to figure out how to do any particular task. To learn a new operation meant a time-consuming search through the flip cards. And whenever something went wrong—a paper jam, say, or a problem with the toner—the machines would flash a cryptic code number, which would require more flipping through the cards to find the corresponding explanation.

In many instances, users would encounter some obstacle, not be able to find out how to resolve it, and simply abandon the machine in midprocedure. The next user to come along, unaware of the previous problem, would assume the machine was broken and call a repair person.

We had to make radical changes in copier design, but it was difficult to sell that message within the company. The idea that there might be serious usability problems with our machines met with resistance in the Xerox development organization that designs our copiers. After all, they had tested their designs against all the traditional human-factors criteria. There was a tendency to assume that any problems with the machines must be the users' fault.

When researchers from PARC began to study the problem, we discovered that the human-factors tests used by the development group didn't accurately reflect how people actually used the machines. So, a PARC anthropologist set up a video camera overlooking one of our new copiers in use at PARC, then had pairs of researchers (including some leading computer scientists) use the machine to do their own copying. The result was dramatic footage of some very smart people, anything but idiots, becoming increasingly frustrated and angry as they tried and failed to figure out how to get the machine to do what they wanted it to do.

The videos proved crucial in convincing the doubters that the company had a serious problem. Even more important, they helped us define what the real problem was. The videos demonstrated that when people use technology like a copier, they construct interpretations of it. In effect, they have a conversation with the machine much as two people have a conversation with each other. But our traditional idiot-proof design provided few cues to help the user interpret what was going on.

We proposed an alternative approach to design. Instead of trying to eliminate trouble, we acknowledged that it was inevitable. So the copier's design should help users manage trouble—just as people manage and recover from misunderstandings during a conversation. This meant keeping the machine as transparent as possible by making it easy for the user to find out what is going on and to discover immediately what to do when something goes wrong.

Xerox's most recent copier families—the 10 and 50 series—reflect this new design principle. Gone are the flip cards of earlier machines. Instead, we include enough computing power in the machines to provide customized instructions on the display panel linked to particular procedures or functions. The information the user receives is immediately put in the context of the task he or she is trying to perform. The new design also incorporates ideas from PARC's research on graphical user interfaces for computers. When something goes wrong, the display panel immediately shows a picture of the machine that visually indicates where the problem is and how to resolve it.

The results of these changes have been dramatic. Where it once took 28 minutes on average to clear a paper jam, it takes 20 seconds with the new design. And because such breakdowns are easier to fix, customers are more tolerant of them when they occur.

Originally published in August 2002
Reprint R0208G

Creativity Is Not Enough

THEODORE LEVITT

Executive Summary

CREATIVITY IS OFTEN TOUTED AS a miraculous road to organizational growth and affluence. But creative new ideas can hinder rather than help a company if they are put forward irresponsibly.

Too often, the creative types who generate a proliferation of ideas confuse creativity with practical innovation. Without understanding the operating executive's day-to-day problems or the complexity of business organizations, they usually pepper their managers with intriguing but short memoranda that lack details about what's at stake or how the new ideas should be implemented. They pass off onto others the responsibility for getting down to brass tacks.

In this classic HBR article from 1963, the author, a professor emeritus at Harvard Business School and a former HBR editor, offers suggestions for the person with a great new idea. First, work with the situation as it is—recognize that the executive is already bombarded with problems. Second, act responsibly by including in your proposal at least a minimal indication of the costs, risks, manpower, and time your idea may involve.

Extolling corporate creativity at the expense of conformity may, in fact, reduce the creative animation of business. Conformity and rigidity are necessary for corporations to function. The purpose of organization is to achieve the order and conformity necessary to do a particular job; without it there would be chaos and decay. And large companies have important attributes that actually facilitate innovation. For one thing, big businesses distribute risk, making it safer for individuals to break new ground. For another, bigness and group decision making function as stabilizers, and stability encourages people to risk presenting ideas that might rock the boat.

Ted Levitt, a former editor of HBR and one of the most incisive commentators on innovation to have appeared in our pages, takes dead aim at the assumption that creativity is superior to conformity. He argues that creativity as it's commonly defined—the ability to come up with brilliantly novel ideas—can actually be destructive to businesses. By failing to take into account practical matters of implementation, big thinkers can inspire organizational cultures dedicated to abstract chatter rather than purposeful action. In such cultures, innovation never happens—because people are always talking about it but never doing it.

Often, the worst thing a company can do, in Levitt's view, is put innovation into the hands of "creative types"— those compulsive idea generators whose distaste for the mundane realities of organizational life renders them incapable of executing any real project. Organizations, by their very nature, are designed to promote order and routine; they are inhospitable environments for innovation. Those who don't understand organizational realities are doomed to see their ideas go unrealized. Only the organizational insider—the apparent conformist—has the practical intelligence to overcome bureaucratic impediments and bring a good idea to a fruitful conclusion.

"CREATIVITY" IS NOT THE miraculous road to business growth and affluence that is so abundantly claimed these days. And for the line manager, particularly, it may be more of a millstone than a milestone. Those who extol the liberating virtues of corporate creativity over the somnambulistic vices of corporate conformity may actually be giving advice that in the end will reduce the creative animation of business. This is because they tend to confuse the getting of ideas with their implementation—that is, confuse creativity in the abstract with practical innovation; not understand the operating executive's day-to-day problems; and underestimate the intricate complexity of business organizations.

The trouble with much of the advice business is getting today about the need to be more vigorously creative is, essentially, that its advocates have generally failed to distinguish between the relatively easy process of being creative in the abstract and the infinitely more difficult process of being innovationist in the concrete. Indeed, they misdefine "creativity" itself. Too often, for them, "creativity" means having great, original ideas. Their emphasis is almost all on the thoughts themselves. Moreover, the ideas are often judged more by their novelty than by their potential usefulness, either to consumers or to the company. In this article, I shall show that in most cases, having a new idea can be "creative" in the abstract but destructive in actual operation, and that often instead of helping a company, it will even hinder it.

Suppose you know two artists. One tells you an idea for a great painting, but he does not paint it. The other has the same idea and paints it. You could easily say the second man is a great creative artist. But could you say the same thing of the first man? Obviously not. He is a talker, not a painter.

That is precisely the problem with so much of today's pithy praise of creativity in business—with the unending flow of speeches, books, articles, and "creativity workshops" whose purpose is to produce more imaginative and creative managers and companies. My observations of these activities over a number of years lead me firmly to this conclusion. They mistake an idea for a great painting with the great painting itself. They mistake brilliant talk for constructive action.

But, as anybody who knows anything about any organization knows only too well, it is hard enough to get things done at all, let alone to introduce a new way of doing things, no matter how good it may seem. A powerful new idea can kick around unused in a company for years, not because its merits are not recognized but because nobody has assumed the responsibility for converting it from words into action. What is often lacking is not creativity in the idea-creating sense but innovation in the action-producing sense, i.e., putting ideas to work.

Ideas Are Not Enough

Why don't we get more innovation?

One of the most repetitious and, I am convinced, most erroneous answers we get to this question is that businessmen are not adequately creative and that they are enslaved by the incubus of conformity. It is alleged that everything in American business would be just dandy if industry were simply more creative and if it would hire more creative people and give them the chance to show their fructifying stuff.

But anybody who carefully looks around in any modern business organization and speaks freely and candidly with the people in it will, I believe, discover something very interesting: namely, there is really very little shortage of creativity and of creative people in American business. The major problem is that so-called creative people often *Many people who are full of ideas simply do not understand how an organization must operate to get things done.* (though certainly not always) pass off on *others* the responsibility for getting down to brass tacks. They have plenty of ideas but little businesslike follow-through. They do not make the right kind of effort to help their ideas get a hearing and a try.

All in all, ideation is relatively abundant. It is its implementation that is more scarce.

Many people who are full of ideas simply do not understand how an organization must operate in order to get things done, especially dramatically new things. All too often, there is the peculiar underlying assumption that creativity automatically leads to actual innovation. In the crippled logic of this line of thinking, ideation (or creativity, if you emphasize the idea-producing aspect of that term) and innovation are treated as synonyms. This kind of thinking is a particular disease of advocates of "brainstorming," who often treat their approach as some sort of ultimate business liberator.[1] Ideation and innovation are not synonyms. The former deals with the generation of ideas; the latter, with their implementation. It is the absence of a constant awareness of this distinction that is responsible for some of the corporate standpattism we see today. (Lest there be any confusion, it is not essential that innovation be successfully implemented to qualify as innovation. The object of the innovation is success, but to require in advance that there be no doubt of its success would disable its chance of ever getting tried.)

The fact that you can put a dozen inexperienced people into a room and conduct a brainstorming session that produces exciting new ideas shows how little relative importance ideas themselves actually have. Almost anybody with the intelligence of the average businessman can produce them, given a halfway decent environment and stimulus. The scarce people are those who have the know-how, energy, daring, and staying power to implement ideas.

Whatever the goals of a business may be, it must make money. To do that, it must get things done. But having ideas is seldom equivalent to getting things done in the business or organizational sense. Ideas do not implement themselves—neither in business nor in art, science, philosophy, politics, love, war. People implement ideas.

A Form of Irresponsibility

Since business is a uniquely "get things done" institution, creativity without action-oriented follow-through is a

uniquely barren form of individual behavior. Actually, in
a sense, it is even irresponsible. This is because: (1) The
creative man who tosses out ideas and does nothing to
help them get implemented is shirking any responsibility
for one of the prime requisites of the business, namely,
action; and (2) by avoiding follow-through, he is behav-
ing in an organizationally intolerable—or, at best,
sloppy—fashion.

The trouble with much creativity today, in my observation, is that many of the people with the ideas have the
peculiar notion that their jobs are finished once the ideas
have been suggested. They believe that it is up to somebody else to work out the dirty details and then implement the proposals. Typically, the more creative the
man, the less responsibility he takes for action. The reason is that the generation of ideas and concepts is often
his sole talent, his stock-in-trade. He seldom has the
energy or staying power, or indeed the interest, to work
with the grubby details that require attention before his
ideas can be implemented.

Anybody can verify this for himself. You need only to
look around in your own company and pick out the two
or three most original idea men in the vicinity. How
many of their ideas can you say they have ever vigorously
and systematically followed through with detailed plans
and proposals for their implementation—even with only
some modest, ballpark suggestions of the risks, the costs,
the manpower requisites, the time budgets, and the possible payout?

The usual situation is that idea men constantly pepper everybody in the organization with proposals and
memoranda that are just brief enough to get attention,
to intrigue, and to sustain interest—but too short to
include any responsible suggestions regarding how the
whole thing is to be implemented and what's at stake. In

some instances it must actually be inferred that they use novel ideas for their disruptive or their self-promotional value. To be more specific:

> *One student of management succession questions whether ideas are always put forth seriously. He suggests that often they may simply be a tactical device to attract attention in order to come first to mind when promotions are made. Hence, ideas are a form of "public relations" within the organization.*[2]

It should be pointed out, however, that something favorable can be said about the relationship of irresponsibility to ideation. The generally effective executive often exhibits what might be called controlled momentary irresponsibility. He recognizes that this attitude is virtually necessary for the free play of imagination. But what distinguishes him is his ability to alternate appropriately between attitudes of irresponsibility and responsibility. He doesn't hold to the former for long—only long enough to make himself more productive.

Psychology of the "Creative Type"

The fact that a consistently highly creative person is generally irresponsible in the way I have used the term is in part predictable from what is known about the freewheeling fantasies of very young children:

> *They are extremely creative, as any kindergarten teacher will testify. They have a naïve curiosity which stumps parents with questions like: "Why can you see through glass?" "Why is there a hole in a doughnut?" "Why is the grass green?" It is this kind of questioning attitude that produces in them so much creative freshness. Yet the unique*

*posture of their lives is their almost total irresponsibility
from blame, work, and the other routine necessities of
organized society. Even the law absolves them from
responsibility for their actions. But all sources testify to
childrens' creativity, even Biblical mythology with its
assertion about wisdom issuing from "the mouths of
babes." More respectable scientific sources have paral-
leled the integrative mechanism of adult creativity with
the childhood thought process that "manifests itself during the preschool period—possibly as early as the appear-
ance of three-word sentences . . ."*[3]

Clinical psychologists have also illustrated what I call
the irresponsibility of creative individuals in Rorschach
and stroboscopic tests. For example:

One analyst says, "Those who took to the Rorschach
like ducks to water, who fantasied and projected freely,
even too freely in some cases, or who could permit themselves to tamper with the form of the blot as given, gave
us our broadest ranges of movement."[4] In short, they
were the least "form-bound," the least inhibited by the
facts of their experience, and hence let their minds
explore new, untried, and novel alternatives to existing
ways of doing things.

The significance of this finding for the analysis of
organizations is pointed up by the observation of another
psychologist that "the theoreticians on the other hand do
not mind living dangerously."[5] The reason is obvious. A
theoretician is not immediately responsible for action. He
is perfectly content to live dangerously because he does so
only on the conceptual level, where he cannot get hurt. To
assume any responsibility for implementation is to risk
dangerous actions, and that can be painfully uncomfort-
able. The safe solution is to steer clear of implementation
and all the dirty work it implies.

The Advice Business

It is to be expected, therefore, that today's most ardent advocates of creativity in business tend to be professional writers, consultants, professors, and often advertising agency executives. Not surprisingly, few of these people have any continuing day-to-day responsibility for the difficult task of implementing powerful new business ideas of a complex nature in the ordinary type of business organization. Few of them have ever had any responsibility for doing work in the conventional kind of complex operating organization. They are not really practicing businessmen in the usual sense. They are literary businessmen. They are the doctors who say, "Do as I say, not as I do," reminiscent of the classic injunction of the boxer's manager, "Get in there and fight. They can't hurt us."

The fact that these people are also so often outspoken about the alleged virulence of conformity in modern business is not surprising. They can talk this way because they have seldom had the nerve to expose themselves for any substantial length of time to the rigorous discipline of an organization whose principal task is not talk but action, not ideas but work.

Impressive sermons are delivered gravely proclaiming the virtues of creativity and the vices of conformity. But so often the authors of these sermons, too, are "outsiders" to the central sector of the business community. Thus, the best-known asserters that American industry is some sort of vast quagmire of quivering conformity—the men who have turned the claim into a tiresome cliché—are people like William H. Whyte, Jr., author of *The Organization Man*,[6] who is a professional writer; Sloan Wilson, author of *The Man in the Gray Flannel*

Suit,[7] who was a college English professor when he wrote the book; and C. Northcote Parkinson (more on him later), also a professor.

Actually, it is not totally fair to condemn this gratuitous crusade of consultants, writers, professors, and the like. American business appears generally to benefit from their existence. Harm is done, however, when the executive fails to consider that the very role of these men absolves them from managerial responsibility. It is hard to accept uncritically the doleful prophesy that so many U.S. companies are hypnotically following each other in a deadly conformist march into economic oblivion. It is hard to accept the tantalizing suggestion that their salvation lies so easily in creativity and that from this will automatically flow profit-building innovation. Perhaps the source of these suggestions should be kept in mind.

The Chronic Complainers

As I have already said, ideation is not a synonym for innovation, conformity is not its simple antonym, and innovation is not the automatic consequence of "creative thinking." Indeed, what some people call conformity in business is less related to the lack of abstract creativity than to the lack of responsible action, whether it be the implementation of new or old ideas.

The proof of this is that in most business organizations, the most continually creative men in the echelons below the executive level—men who are actively discontent with the here and now and are full of suggestions about what to do about it—are also generally known as corporate malcontents. They tend to be complaining constantly about the standpat senility of the

management, about its refusal to see the obvious facts
of its own massive inertia. They complain about
management refusing to do the things that have been
suggested to it for years. They often complain that
management does not even want creative ideas, that
ideas rock the boat (which they do), and that management is interested more in having a smoothly running
(or is it smoothly ruining?) organization than in a
rapidly forward-vaulting business.

In short, they talk about the company being a fester-
ing sore of deadly conformity, full of decaying vegetables
who systematically oppose new ideas with the old ideolo-
gies. And then, of course, they frequently quote their
patron saint, William H. Whyte, Jr., with all his misin-
formed moralizing and his conjectural evidence about
what goes on inside an operating organization. (Whyte's
fanciful notions of such operations have recently been
demolished by the careful studies of the veteran student
of social organization W. Lloyd Warner in his *The Corporation in the Emergent American Society.*[8])

Why Doors Are Closed

The reason the creative malcontent speaks this way is
that so often the people to whom he addresses his flow of
ideas do, indeed, after a while, ignore him and tell him to
go away. They shut their doors to his endless entreaties;
they refuse to hear his ideas any longer. Why? There is a
plausible explanation.

The reason the executive so often rejects new ideas is
that he is a busy man whose chief day-in, day-out task is
to handle an ongoing stream of problems. He receives an
unending flow of questions on which decisions must be
made. Constantly he is forced to deal with problems to

which solutions are more or less urgent and the answers to which are far from clear-cut. It may seem splendid to a subordinate to supply his boss with a lot of brilliant new ideas to help him in his job. But advocates of creativity must once and for all understand the pressing facts of the executive's life: Every time an idea is submitted to him, it creates more problems for him—and he already has enough.

Advocates of creativity must understand the pressing facts of the executive's life: Every time an idea is submitted to him, it creates more problems for him—and he already has enough.

My colleague, Professor Raymond A. Bauer, has pointed out an instructive example from another field of activity. He notes that many congressmen and senators have the opportunity to have a political science intern assigned to "help" them. However, some congressmen and senators refuse this "help" on the grounds that these interns generate so many ideas that they disrupt the legislator's regular business.

Making Ideas Useful

Yet innovation is necessary in business—and innovation begins with somebody's proposal. What is the answer for the man with a new idea? I have two thoughts to offer:

1. **He must work with the situation as it is.** Since the executive is already constantly bombarded with problems, there is little wonder that after a while he does not want any more new ideas. The "idea man" must learn to accept this as a fact of life and act accordingly.

2. When he suggests an idea, the responsible procedure is to include at least some minimal indication
of what it involves in terms of costs, risks, manpower, time, and perhaps even specific people who
ought to carry it through. That *is* responsible behavior, because it makes it easier for the executive to
evaluate the idea and because it raises fewer problems. That *is* the way creative thinking will more
likely be converted into innovation.

It will be argued, of course, that to saddle the creative
individual with the responsibility of spelling out the
details of implementation would curb or even throttle
his unique talent. This is probably true. But this could be
salutary, both for him and for the company. Ideas are
useless unless used. The proof of their value is their
implementation. Until then they are in limbo. If the executive's job pressures mean that an idea seldom gets a
good hearing unless it is responsibly presented, then the
unthrottled and irresponsible creative man is use-less to
the company. If an insistence on some responsibility for
implementation throttles him, he may produce fewer
ideas, but their chances of a judicious hearing and therefore of being followed through are greatly improved. The
company will benefit by trying the ideas, and the creative
man will benefit by getting the satisfaction of knowing
he is being listened to. He will not have to be a malcontent any more.

Deciding Factors

This is not to suggest that every idea needs a thoroughly
documented study before it is mentioned to anyone. Far
from it. What is needed will vary from case to case
depending on four factors:

The Position or Rank of the Idea Originator in the Organization. How "responsible" a man needs to act for an idea to get a hearing clearly depends on his rank.

The powerful chief executive officer can simply instruct subordinates to take and develop one of his ideas. That is enough to give it a hearing and perhaps even implementation. To that extent, talk *is* virtually action. Similarly, the head of a department can do the same thing in his domain. But when the ideas flow in the opposite direction—upward instead of downward—they are unlikely to flow unless they are supported by the kind of follow-through I have been urging.

The Complexity of the Idea. The more complex and involved the implications of an idea, and the more change and rearrangement it may require within the organization or in its present way of doing things, then obviously the greater is the need to cover the required ground in some responsible fashion when the proposal is presented.

But I do not suggest that the "how to" questions need to be covered as thoroughly and carefully as would be required by, say, a large corporation's executive committee when it finally decides whether to implement or drop the suggestion. Such a requirement would be so rigid that it might dry up all ideas because their originators simply would not have the time, competence, or staff help to go to that much effort.

The Nature of the Industry. How much supporting detail a subordinate should submit along with his idea often depends on the industry involved and the intent of the idea.

One reason there is such a high premium put on "creativity" in advertising is because the first requisite of an ad is to get attention. Hence "creativity" frequently revolves around the matter of trying to achieve visual or auditory impact such that the ad stands out above the constantly expanding stream of advertising noise to which the badgered consumer is subjected. To this extent, in the advertising industry, being "creative" is quite a different thing, by and large, from what it is, say, in the steel industry. Putting an eye patch on the man in the Hathaway shirt is "no sooner said than done." The idea is virtually synonymous with its implementation. But in the steel industry, an idea, say, to change the discount structure to encourage users of cold, rolled sheet steel to place bigger but fewer orders is so full of possible complications and problems that talk is far from being action or even a program for action. To get even a sympathetic first hearing, such an idea needs to be accompanied by a good deal of factual and logical support.

The Attitude and Job of the Person to Whom the Idea Is Submitted. Everybody knows that some bosses are more receptive to new ideas than others. Some are more receptive to extreme novelty than others. The extent of their known receptiveness will in part determine the elaborateness of support a suggested new idea requires at its original stage.

But, equally important, it is essential to recognize that the greater the pressures of day-to-day operating responsibilities on the executive, the more resistance he is likely to have to new ideas. If the operating burden happens to fall on him, his job is to make the present setup work smoothly and well. A new idea requires change, and change upsets the smooth (or perhaps faltering) regularity of the present operation on whose effectiveness he is being judged and on which his career future depends. He has very good reason to be extremely careful about a new proposal. He needs lots of good risk-reducing reasons before he will look at one very carefully.

What his actual requirements are will also depend on the attitudes of his superiors to risk taking and mis takes. In one company I am familiar with, the two most senior officers have a unique quality of enormous receptivity to novelty—sometimes the wilder the proposal, the better. The result is that new ideas, no matter how vaguely stated or extreme, get sympathetic and quick hearings throughout all levels of the company. But this is a rare organization for two reasons.

First, the chairman is now about 40 years old. He became president when he was 28, having been selected by his predecessor as the heir apparent when he was about 24. He vaulted quickly from one top job to another, never really having to spend very much time "making good" in the conventional sense in a difficult day-to-day operating job at a low level. Virtually his entire career was one of high-level responsibility where his ideas could be passed down to a corps of subordinates for detailed examination and evaluation. These experiences taught him the value of wild ideation without his having to risk his rise to the top by seeming to suggest irresponsible projects.

Second, the present president of this same company came in as a vice president, also at 28, and directly from an advertising agency. His career experiences were similar to the chairman's.

It is easy for both of these men to be permissive, in part because they have never really had to risk their climb up the hierarchical ladder by seeming to shoot wild. They always had teams of subordinates to check their ideas and willing superiors to listen to them. Anybody who has not had this history or conditioning will find it extremely hard to change once he gets very far up the corporate pecking order.

In short, a permissive, open, risk-taking environment cannot be created simply by the good intentions of the top management. The reason is either that high-level executives who have got to their top posts by a lifetime of judicious executive behavior are incapable of changing their habits or that, if their habits are changed, their subordinates will not believe they really mean it. And in lots of small ways, they see the justification of their disbeliefs.

Need for Discipline

Writers on the subject of creativity and innovation invariably emphasize the essential primacy of the creative impulse itself. Almost as an afterthought they talk about the necessity of teaching people to sell their ideas and of stimulating executives to listen to the ideas of subordinates and peers. Then they often go on casually to make some "do-gooder" statement about the importance of creating a permissive organizational climate for creative people. They rarely try to look at the executive's job and suggest how the creative genius might alter his behavior to suit the boss's requirements. It is always the boss who is being told to mend his ways. The reason for their one-sided siding with the creative man is that they are often hostile, just as he is, to the idea of "the organization" itself. They actively dislike organizations, but they seldom know exactly why.

I think I know the reason. It is that organization and creativity do not seem to go together, while organization and conformity do. Advocacy of a "permissive environment" for creativity in an organization is often a veiled attack on the idea of the organization itself. This quickly becomes clear when one recognizes this inescapable fact: One of the collateral purposes of an organization *is* to be inhospitable to a great and constant flow of ideas and creativity.

Whether we are talking about the U.S. Steel Corporation or the United Steelworkers of America, the U.S. Army or the Salvation Army, the United States or the U.S.S.R., the purpose of organization is to achieve the kind and degree of order and conformity necessary to do a particular job. The organization exists to restrict and channel the range of individual actions and behavior into a predictable and knowable routine. Without organization there would be chaos and decay. Organization exists in order to create that amount and kind of inflexibility that are necessary to get the most pressingly intended job done efficiently and on time.

Creativity and innovation disturb that order. Hence, organization tends to be inhospitable to creativity and innovation, though without creativity and innovation it would eventually perish. That is why small, one-man shops are so often more animated and "innovationary" than large ones. They have virtually no organization (precisely because they are one-man shops) and often are run by self-willed autocrats who act on impulse.

Organizations are created to achieve order. They have policies, procedures, and formal or powerfully informal (unspoken) rules. The job for which the organization exists could not possibly get done without these rules, procedures, and policies. And these produce the so-called conformity that is so blithely deprecated by the critics of the organization and life inside it.

Parkinson's Flaw

It is not surprising that C. Northcote Parkinson and his *Parkinson's Law* enjoy such an admiring following among teachers, writers, consultants, and professional social critics. Most of these people have carefully chosen as their own professions work that keeps them as far as modern society lets anyone get from the rigorous taskmaster of the organization. Most of them more or less lead a sort of one-man, self-employed existence in which there are few make-or-break postmortems of their activities. They live pretty much in autonomous isolation. Many of them, I suspect, have avoided life in the organization because they are incapable of submitting to its rigid discipline. Parkinson has provided them a way in which they can laugh at the majority, who *do* submit to the organization, and feel superior rather than oppressed, as minorities usually do.

It is also not surprising (indeed it is quite expected) that Parkinson himself should be anything but an organization man—that he is a teacher of history, a painter, and, of all things, a historian on warfare in the Eastern Seas. This is about as far as you can get from the modern landbound organization. Parkinson's writings have in recent years brought him into such continuing contact with business that he has now decided to go into business himself. In doing so, he has proved the truth of all that I have been saying: The business he has decided to enter is, of course, the consulting business!

Parkinson is very entertaining. The executive who cannot laugh along with him probably is too paranoid to be trusted with a responsible job. But most of today's blithe cartoonists of the organization would be impoverished for material were they not blessed with an enormous ignorance of the facts of organizational life. Let me put it as emphatically as I can. A company cannot function as an anarchy. It must be organized, it must be routinized, it must be planned in some way in the various stages of its operation. That is why we have so many organizations of so many different kinds. And to the extent that operations planning is needed, we get rigidity, order, and therefore some amount of conformity. No organization can have everybody running off uncoordinated in several different directions at once. There must be rules and standards.

Where there are enough rules, there will be damn fool rules. These can be mercilessly cartooned. But some rules which to an expert on ancient naval history look foolish are far from foolish if he bothers to learn about the problems of the business, or the government, or whatever group the particular organization is designed to deal with.

From Creativity to Innovation

All this raises a seemingly frightening question. If conformity and rigidity are necessary requisites of organization, and if these in turn help stifle creativity, and furthermore if the creative man might indeed be stifled if he is required to spell out the details needed to convert his ideas into effective innovations, does all this mean that modern organizations have evolved into such involuted monsters that they must suffer the fearful fate of the dinosaur—too big and unwieldy to survive?

The answer to this is *no*. First, it is questionable whether the creative impulse would automatically dry up if the idea man is required to take some responsibility for follow-through. The people who so resolutely proclaim their own creative energy will scarcely assert that they need a hothouse for its flowering. Secondly, the large organization has some important attributes that actually facilitate innovation. Its capacity to distribute risk over its broad economic base and among the many individuals involved in implementing newness are significant. They make it both economically and, for the individuals involved, personally easier to break untried ground.

Ideas are useless unless used. The proof of their value is their implementation. Until then they are in limbo.

What often misleads people is that making big operating or policy changes requires also making big organizational changes. Yet it is precisely one of the great virtues of a big organization that, in the short run at least, its momentum is irreversible and its organizational structure is, for all practical purposes, nearly impenetrable. A vast machinery exists to get a certain job done. That job must continue to get the toughest kind of serious attention, no matter how exotically revolutionary a big operating or policy change may be. The boat can and may have to be rocked, but one virtue of a big boat is that it takes an awful lot to rock it. Certain people or departments in the boat may feel the rocking more than others and to that extent strive to avoid the incidents that produce it. But the built-in stabilizers of bigness and of group decision making can be used as powerful influences in *encouraging* people to risk these incidents.

Finally, the large organization has an organizational alternative to the alleged "conservatizing" consequences of bigness. There is some evidence that the relatively rigid organization can build into its own structure certain flexibilities which would provide an organizational home for the creative but irresponsible individual. What may be required, especially in the large organization, is not so much a suggestion-box system as a specialized group whose function is to receive ideas, work them out, and follow them through in the necessary manner. This would be done after the group has evaluated each idea and, preferably, spoken at length with its originator. Then when the idea and the necessary follow-through are passed on to the appropriate executive, he will be more willing to listen. To illustrate:

- An organizational setup that approximates this structure has been established in the headquarters Marketing Department of the Mobil Oil Company.[9]

- A similar approach exists at the Schering Corporation under the name Management R&D. Its purpose is to nurture and develop new ideas and new methods of decision making.[10]

- Another suggestion which takes less solidly tangible organizational form in practice has been made by Murray D. Lincoln, president of Nationwide Insurance Company. He makes a plea for the notion of a company having a *Vice President in Charge of Revolution*.[11]

Beyond these, the problems and needs of companies differ. To this extent, they may have to find their own special ways of dealing with the issues discussed in this article. The important point is to be conscious of the possible need or value of some system of making creativity yield more innovation.

Some companies have greater need for such measures than others have. And, as pointed out earlier, the need hinges in part on the nature of the industry. Certainly it is easier to convert creativity into innovation in the advertising business than it is in an operating company with elaborate production processes, long channels of distribution, and a complex administrative setup.

For those critics of and advisers to U.S. industry who repeatedly call for more creativity in business, it is well to try first to understand the profound distinction between creativity and innovation and then perhaps to spend a little more time calling on creative individuals to take added responsibility for implementation. The fructifying potentials of creativity vary enormously with the particular industry, with the climate in the organization, with the organizational level of the idea man, and with the kinds of day-in, day-out problems, pressures, and responsibilities of the man to whom he addresses his ideas. Without clearly appreciating these facts, those who declare that a company will somehow grow and prosper merely by having more creative people make a fetish of their own illusions.

Notes

1. See, for instance, Alex F. Osborn, *Applied Imagination: Principles and Procedures of Creative Thinking* (New York, Charles Scribner's Sons, 1953).

2. See Bernard Levenson, "Bureaucratic Succession," in *Complex Organizations: A Sociological Reader*, edited by Amitai Etzioni (New York, Rinehart & Company, 1961).

3. See Stanley Stark, "Mills, Mannheim, and the Psychology of Knowledge," mimeographed (Urbana, University of Illinois, 1960).

4. G.S. Klein, "The Personal World Through Perception," in *Perception: An Approach to Personality*, edited by R.R. Blake and G.V. Ramsey (New York, The Ronald Press, 1951). For more on "the creative personality," see Morris I. Stein and Shirley J. Heinze, *Creativity and the Individual* (Glencoe, Illinois, The Free Press, 1960).

5. Herbert Feigl, "Philosophical Embarrassments of Psychology," *American Psychologist*, March 1959.

6. New York, Simon & Schuster, 1956.

7. New York, Simon & Schuster, 1955.

8. New York, Harper & Brothers, 1962.

9. For a detailed discussion of how such a setup might operate and be organized, see my *Innovation in Marketing* (New York, McGraw-Hill, 1962).

10. See Victor M. Longstreet, "Management R & D," HBR July–August 1961.

11. New York, McGraw-Hill, 1960.

Originally published in August 2002
Reprint R0208K

About the Contributors

TERESA M. AMABILE is the Edsel Bryant Ford Professor of Business Administration and Head of the Entrepreneurial Management Unit at Harvard Business School. Originally educated and employed as a chemist, Dr. Amabile received her Ph.D. in psychology from Stanford University in 1977. Dr. Amabile's research encompasses team creativity and organizational innovation. This twenty-five-year program of research on how the work environment can influence creativity and motivation has yielded a theory of creativity and innovation; methods for assessing creativity, motivation, and the work environment; and a set of prescriptions for maintaining and stimulating innovation. Dr. Amabile is the author of *Creativity in Context* and *Growing Up Creative*, as well as over 100 scholarly papers, chapters, and presentations. She serves on the editorial boards of *Academy of Management Journal*, *Creativity Research Journal*, *Creativity and Innovation Management*, and *Journal of Creative Behavior*.

MARTHA CRAUMER is a business writer based in Cambridge, MA. Working at her dining room table, she develops and edits articles, white papers, marketing collateral, video scripts, and Web site content—when not otherwise distracted by the TV, the outdoors, or the refrigerator. In a previous life she was a Hong Kong banker. Prior to that she lived for a short time in France, where she developed an ongoing love affair with wine, cheese, and good food. To offset her tendency to overindulge, she works out vigorously. She also loves reading, traveling, movies, competitive backgammon, and lazing about doing as little as possible.

At the time this article was originally published, PETER F. DRUCKER was the Marie Rankin Clarke Professor of Social Science and Management at Claremont Graduate University's Peter F. Drucker Graduate School of Management in Claremont, CA.

CONSTANCE N. HADLEY is a doctoral candidate in the Organizational Behavior Program at Harvard Business School. She holds a B.A. in Social Psychology from Princeton University and an M.B.A. from the Wharton School. Her previous employers include General Mills and McKinsey & Company.

At the time this article was originally published, STEVEN J. KRAMER was an independent researcher and writer based in Wayland, MA.

At the time this article was originally published, THEODORE LEVITT was Professor Emeritus of marketing at Harvard Business School.

At the time this article was originally published, ANDRALL E. PEARSON was a professor of business administration at Harvard Business School in Boston, MA. After becoming Professor Emeritus, he served as the Chairman and CEO of Tricon Global Restaurants, the world's largest restaurant chain.

ELLEN PEEBLES is a Senior Editor at *Harvard Business Review.*

JOHN SEELY BROWN was the Chief Scientist of Xerox Corporation until April 2002 and was also the director of the Xerox Palo Alto Research Center (PARC) until June 2000—a position he held for twelve years. While head of PARC, Brown expanded the role of corporate research to include such topics as organizational learning, complex adaptive systems, micro electrical mechanical system (MEMS), and NANO technology. His personal research interests include digital culture, ubiquitous computing, web service architectures, and organizational and individual learning.

JOHN D. WOLPERT leads IBM's Austin Extreme Blue Lab, a unique incubator for talent, technology, and business innovation. Extreme Blue deploys teams of top business and technical talent worldwide on projects that explore emerging opportunities for IBM. John has been a strategy consultant, a chief marketing officer, a software developer, a business owner, and a theater director. He has worked for and consulted to a variety of firms, including IBM, Apple Computer, Pacific Bell, MCI, and The Washington Post Company. He is an alumnus of UC Berkeley and received his M.B.A. from Georgetown University. He is currently writing a book on corporate innovation and can be reached at jwolpert@us.ibm.com or through his web site, www.inter-firm.com.

Index